infidelity recovery 101

How to Heal from an Affair

Save Your Marriage after Infidelity and Rebuild Your Relationship

The Comprehensive Guide to Overcoming Sexual Betrayal

Barbarah Gotman

The journey toward healing begins with acknowledging the pain,

Yet it flourishes with the inner strength to conquer it

The
Golden
Scar

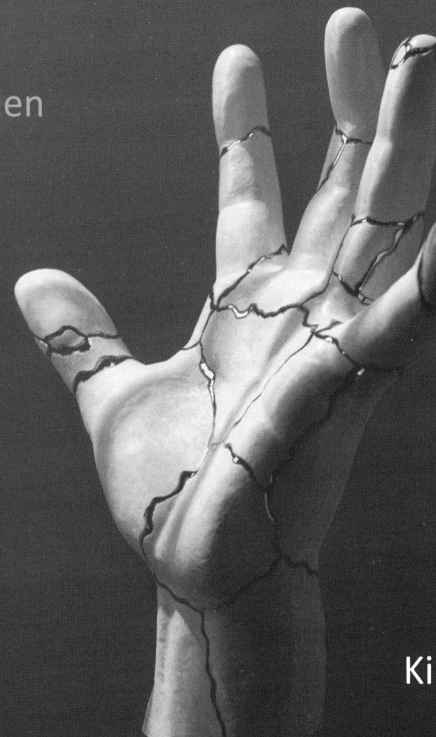

Kintsugi

Jars based on the Concept of Kintsugi

Embracing the Golden Scars of Infidelity

Welcome to the captivating world of "Infidelity Recovery 101". This compelling piece consists of evocative imagery- portraying a couple carrying each other's weight during their journey towards healing even though they are covered with visible scars witnessed due to infidelity- while still holding onto hope despite their broken relationship.

Our cover design derives inspiration from an ancient Japanese artwork called "Kintsugi," which some call "the golden scar." Originally derived from Zen philosophy, Kintsugi includes repairing broken ceramics using lacquer mixed with gold, silver, or platinum without attempting to cover up or disguising the tiles' cracks or flaws; in this manner, Kintsugi celebrates and transforms damages and imperfections into something extraordinary. In recovering from infidelity issues, an analogy between relationships and Kintsugi stands for hope.

Though betrayals may permanently damage relationships when couples work together through mutual healing practices such as dedicated effort and communication efforts, these scars can inevitably transform into golden bonds more robust than ever. We must remember that healing involves embracing imperfections rather than denying them while acknowledging that every defect is integral to a relationship's narrative story. Suppose you incorporate the Kintsugi concept into modern-day settings to aid infidelity recovery on your journey toward transformation. In that case, you'll experience unparalleled power while learning to rebuild trust and practical communication tools while strengthening intimacy bonds like never before.

Each chapter in this publication be-aims focuses on moving forward by cultivating practical strategies designed using innovative techniques to successfully guide readers through their journey. This insightful guide comes packed with valuable expertise and creative exercises to prompt some thought-provoking moments worthy of conversation between couples. These well-crafted exercises aim to empower partners in setting on the path of healing after experiencing infidelity by providing them with empathy & openness while encouraging heartfelt discussions that will accelerate their journey toward regaining trust in one another. Partners embarking on this journey will derive maximum fulfillment if they approach each page in reverence, looking forward to uncovering emotional depths.

Remember always that even though such cases come with their difficulties, this book serves as an illuminating beam offering the tools and support to overcome them. Wishing you a fulfilling transformative experience as you turn these pages.

Infidelity Recovery 101

Contents

Introduction

Affair recovery is the most common way of recuperating a relationship intellectually, inwardly, and truly after it has encountered disloyalty. Affair recovery generally takes somewhere in the range of a half year to two years. In many cases, it is a problematic cycle yet a potential one for couples with lowliness, sympathy, and steadiness. An affair can be anywhere, from a close-to-home affair to a sexual affair. A profound affair is when you foster an improperly close-to-home connection with somebody other than your life partner. That individual turns into your dearest companion, your perfect partner. You share everything with them, and you begin going gaga for them. With a profound affair, it's inevitable before it turns sexual, except if it's halted. A sexual affair is a point at which there's sexual contact. Due to the connection, close-to-home affairs are usually more complex to recuperate from than casual hookups. A solid relationship is framed in a profound affair that can be challenging to break.

Conversely, a casual hookup frequently includes practically no connection, so breaking is much more straightforward. All types of affairs are profoundly horrible to relationships across the globe. The main thing that stones the underpinning of safety in a relationship is unfaithfulness. Regardless of what language you speak, regardless of what shade of your skin, regardless of what nationality or social foundation, unfaithfulness shakes the groundwork of relationships like nothing else. The sold-out accomplice usually creates side effects likened to PTSD, Post Horrendous Pressure Problem, due to the considerable aggravation and loss of control. A ton of the side effects can include nosy contemplations, peevishness, fits of anxiety, flashbacks, numbness to life, etc. The accompanying advances are intended to assist your relationship with recuperating.

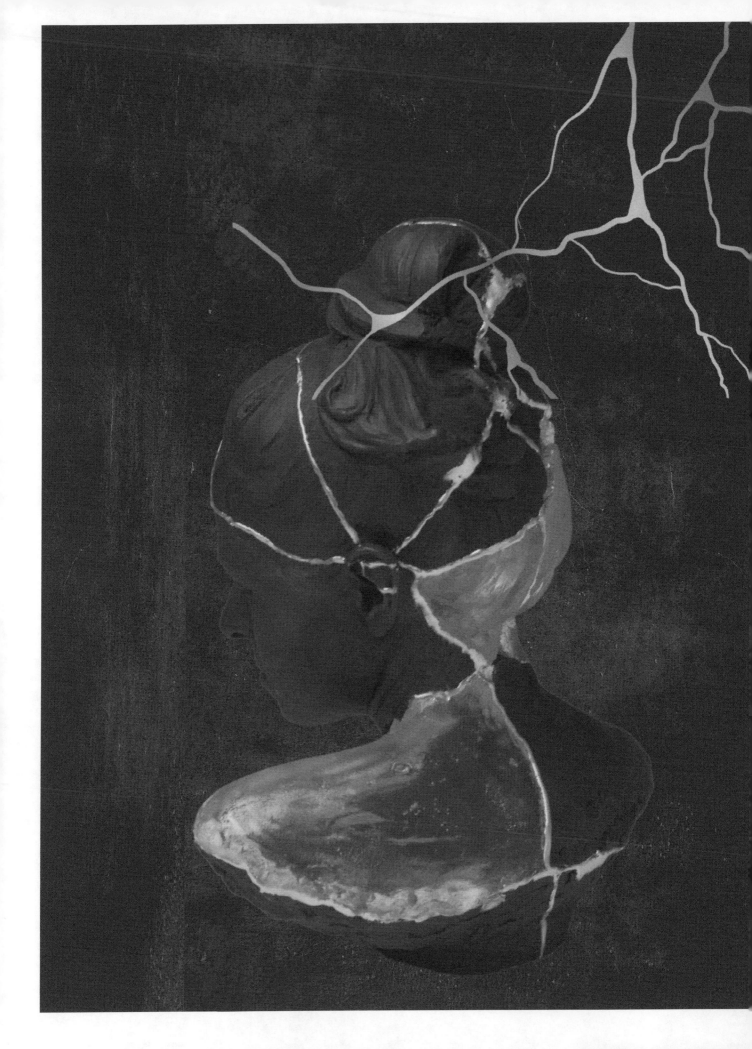

Why do affairs occur?

Unfaithfulness can occur in a wide range of relationships. That incorporates relationships that appear to be content and those with numerous issues. Treachery might occur because of an assortment of factors, including:

- Absence of warmth.
- Loss of affection, love, and care for one another.
- Feeble obligation to the relationship.
- Breakdown of correspondence about close-to-home and relationship needs.
- Low confidence.
- Actual medical problems, like persistent torment or handicap.
- Emotional well-being issues, like sorrow or nervousness.
- Dependence, like dependence on liquor, sex, sentiment, or medications.
- Issues that aren't tended to in a marriage, like anxiety toward closeness or keeping away from the struggle.
- Significant life-altering events include becoming guardians or kids venturing out from home.
- Distressing periods, for example, when life partners should be separated for.

Discovering an affair

The point when an affair is uncovered frequently sets off solid feelings for the two accomplices. The accomplice who has been undermined could feel damaged by the double-crossing of trust and loss of profound wellbeing. The accomplice with the illicit relationship could expect they won't ever be pardoned. At the point when an affair is first found, it very well may be challenging to figure obviously to the end of going with long-haul choices. Think about making the accompanying strides:

Try not to pursue unwise choices. If you could genuinely hurt yourself or another person, seek a clinical expert's help immediately.

Give each other space. The disclosure of an affair can be extraordinary. As you attempt to get a handle on what has occurred, you could wind up acting in unusual ways of doing things that you usually wouldn't. Give yourself and your accomplice some time. Attempt to avoid genuinely charged conversations as you start the recuperating system.

Look for help. It can assist with imparting your experience and sentiments to believed companions or friends and family who support and energize you. Stay away from individuals who will, more often than not, be critical, fundamental, or one-sided.

Take as much time as is needed. Even though you could want to comprehend what has occurred, don't delve into the personal subtleties of the affair immediately. Doing such without the direction of an expert, like a marriage mentor, may be destructive.

Stage One-Stop all contact

The initial step is to shut down all contact with the individual with whom you've had the illicit relationship. That might require different things. Contingent upon your circumstance, this might incorporate leaving your place of employment, moving to an alternate area or state, evolving houses of worship, and so forth. You need to remove all contact with the affair individual since, supposing that you don't, the affair will wait. Many individuals are under the misguided judgment that they can stop the affair yet simultaneously be companions with the individual or still see them once in for a spell. That is incomprehensible. An affair is a fixation. The vibe of significant synthetic compounds in your cerebrum was low due to things happening in your life and your marriage. Then, this individual approached and addressed your issues and overflowed your cerebrum with feel-great synthetic substances, transforming them into dependence. Very much like any dependence, whether it's heroin or cocaine or whatever, assuming you get around it, you will fall once more into it, moreover with affairs. Assuming you've taken part in an extramarital entanglement with someone, that individual has turned into your fixation, so considering that you interact with them on any level doubtlessly, you will fall right once again into the affair. Also, each time you have rehashed contact with the illicit relationship, it will traumatize your companion, and all mending in your marriage will be lost.

Suppose you're the sold-out accomplice understanding this, and your accomplice won't end all contact with their darling. In that case, your most memorable round of offense is to open the affair to all your loved ones, making it difficult for your accomplice to end it. The expectation isn't to disgrace your accomplice but to have confided in family and companions, go up against them about their harmful behavior, to snap them back into the real world. At the point when you're in an affair, you frequently don't understand how wrecking your way of behaving is because you're carrying on with a dream. If that prevalent difficulty doesn't make your accomplice end all contact with their darling, your best course of action ought to be division with no connection until your accomplice can't demonstrate they have any more extended contact with their sweetheart. This is significant for two reasons. First, it permits you to lay out a limit so you're not constantly sincerely manhandled by your accomplice's continuous contact with their darling. Second, it allows your accomplice to see what existence without you would be like. On the off chance that following 3-6 months, your accomplice hasn't finished all contact with their darling, then continue with separate.

The delinquent accomplice should also accept a sexually transmitted disease test if they contracted something during the affair. The sold-out accomplice must go with them so that the outcomes might be able to hear firsthand. This ought to be required regardless of whether the unruly accomplice guarantees it was a profound affair and nothing physical occurred. You would instead not take any risks. The main thing more regrettable than recuperating from an experience is getting a sexually transmitted disease from your accomplice due to their affair.

Stage Two-Open all records

Step two is to impart all records and your telephone to your accomplice to show you have no more contact with your darling. This is also suggested for couples with no treachery to cultivate trust and straightforwardness. It conveys I don't have anything to stow away. It would be best if you willfully give your telephone over at whatever point your companion wants. You've broken trust. To procure that trust back, you need to open up all records. Some of the time, having secret accounts can entice. Yet, assuming that you genuinely believe your marriage should recuperate, it's an exercise in futility to have any mysteries. It would be best if you turned everything over. It will help your double-crossed mate gradually begin confiding in you again because your assertion amounts to nothing right now. You've broken trust; you've lied. What you say doesn't make any difference. Your activities matters. Deliberately opening up all records and offering your telephone to your accomplice will assist them with beginning to mend. They can't begin the mending journey until they realize you have no more contact with your darling. Rehearsing receptiveness likewise helps the unruly accomplice since affairs flourish in mystery. Along these lines, assuming there's no a potential open door for it to fill in mystery it will ultimately kick the bucket.

Assuming that your accomplice denies or is irate about sharing all records and their telephone to demonstrate they have no more contact with their sweetheart recall the two stages of offense above. Open the affair to all loved ones to make prevailing difficulty and in the event that that is insufficient for them to participate get a partition until they do. Assuming your accomplice is furious or safe about imparting everything to you it's presumably on the grounds that they are attempting to keep in contact with their sweetheart and don't have any desire to end it.

One method for contemplating affairs is the individual who ventures outside the marriage and has the illicit relationship, that is 100 percent their shortcoming. In any case, the environment in the marriage that made them defenseless to venturing outside the marriage is typically both accomplice's shortcoming

Stage Three-Show regret

Stage three is you need to show genuine regret. On the off chance that you've engaged in extramarital relations, act impassive toward the effect it's had on your life partner, recovery is beyond the realm of possibilities. You need to take possession for how wrecking this has been to your relationship. Regardless of whether you were despondent, regardless of whether your necessities weren't being met, you broke your commitments to your mate and double-crossed them. Consequently, it's basic to take possession for the amount you have shaken the groundwork of your marriage. Sincere regret for having the illicit relationship is fundamental. On the off chance that you don't take proprietorship for the affair and aren't sorry, it will be close to unimaginable for your accomplice to excuse you.

Stage Four - Interaction the damages

Stage four is handling through your damages, which might head the two paths. Clearly the sold out companion will have a ton of harmed they'll have to communicate. In any case, the delinquent accomplice may likewise have harms in light of the fact that maybe one reason they had the illicit relationship is their requirements were neglected over and again for a really long time notwithstanding their regular protests. So both of you want a strategy to get out your damages. I show couples a compromise technique called the rejoin device, which is a bunch of rules on the most proficient method to guard discussions. At the point when the hurt isn't completely vented and delivered, it will turn out in damaging ways through shouting, brutal remarks, and derisive comments, which will just exacerbate the situation. Hurt individuals hurt individuals however that simply harms the relationship further. Thus, having some sort of technique to manage your damages valuably is critical. You might have to work with a relationship mentor to do this really.

Stage Five-Examine the subtleties

Individuals frequently can't help thinking about how much detail ought to be shared about an affair. A few sold out mates need to know everything about others just need a rundown. Normally the unruly companion would rather not share any subtleties, so the deceived mate continues to request them, at times for a really long time. Each time the affair gets raised, it re-damages the relationship. The deceived companion ought to be accountable for how much detail is shared, not the rebellious mate. Be that as it may, recollect the more detail you hear the more crushed you might turn into. In this manner, consider cautiously how much data you want to be aware and why. Cause a rundown of the relative multitude of inquiries you to have about the illicit relationship for your unpredictable accomplice. A solicitation their unruly life partner to respond to the inquiries while associated with a falsehood identifier test to expand the reliability of their responses. That is an individual choice up to the sold out accomplice. In the event that you're the rebellious accomplice, your responsibility is to work a lot harder at recuperating the marriage than your life partner so assuming they demand an untruth finder test, make it happen! Be that as it may, after the inquiries, the two accomplices ought to make a deal to avoid raising the affair any longer, barring triggers, on the grounds that each time it's raised the marriage will endure.

Stage Six-Oversee triggers

Some portion of Post-Awful Pressure Problem (PTSD) is getting set off. The people who have been in battle will frequently encounter flashbacks of the abhorrence they went through. The individuals who have experienced cataclysmic events will frequently encounter flashbacks of the annihilation they encountered. In like manner, the people who have been double-crossed by an illicit relationship will frequently have flashbacks of the aggravation they endured. Along these lines, figuring out how to oversee triggers is significant for all couples who have encountered an illicit relationship. At the point when set off, the deceived companion should keep away from two limits. The first isn't referencing the trigger and experiencing peacefully, which will make you withdrawal inwardly. The second is turning out to be verbally forceful toward your accomplice, which will prompt clash. The third and prescribed approach is to communicate each trigger with your delicate underside. The delicate underside is the delicate sentiments under your displeasure, for example, miserable, hurt, shaky, unfortunate, and so on. For instance, a delicate underside proclamation when set off could be "I was watching a film the previous evening that elaborate an affair and it set off me with your affair and raised every one of the sensations of trouble, hurt, and dread." The occupation of the delinquent companion is to answer with sympathy, a statement of regret, and consolation, for example, "I can perceive how the film would have set off your sensations of misery, hurt, and dread with the affair and Please accept my apologies I hurt you, and I guarantee at absolutely no point ever to follow through with something like that in the future." This kind of reaction to triggers sets out recuperating open doors for the marriage and assuming took care of in this manner triggers will diminish with time. The inverse is additionally obvious. Assuming the double-crossed accomplice communicates triggers with outrage and the unpredictable accomplice answers with preventiveness, triggers will increment with time.

Stage Seven-Foster sympathy

Stage seven is creating sympathy toward your accomplice's terrible way of behaving. Chipping away at empathy is stage seven since it's just suitable after the unruly accomplice has removed all contact with their sweetheart, opened all records, communicated genuine regret, has listened really to your damages, has helped out addressing your inquiries concerning the affair, and has answered well to your triggers. Really at that time does it check out to begin dealing with sympathy toward their terrible way of behaving. Creating empathy doesn't pardon away their terrible way of behaving yet it makes sense of why it happened. There are four inquiries to respond to cultivate empathy toward your accomplice's pernicious way of behaving and it's essential to audit these four regions at whatever point your hurt ascents. To start with, shouldn't something be said about your accomplice's childhood or past might have impacted their illicit relationship? For instance, numerous grown-ups brought up in a home where they felt deficient are at higher gamble for an affair on the grounds that an affair causes them to feel very needed and significant. Second, what might be said about your accomplice's conditions might have impacted their illicit relationship? For instance, the more pressure individuals are under the less resolution they need to oppose enticing circumstances. Third, what was your example of conduct that might have expanded their helplessness to an affair? For instance, maybe you had been keeping away from close to home or actual closeness for a drawn out timeframe. Fourth, what might be said about your past is getting initiated by the affair? For instance, maybe you have a past filled with feeling dismissed or deserted growing up so that is increasing your response to the affair. The objective of the inquiries is to assist you with seeing every one of the factors that added to the affair. In the event that you don't see every one of the factors, it's challenging to push ahead. Evaluating the solutions to the four inquiries frequently goes about as balm to the affair wound when it ascends by developing sympathy.

Stage Eight-Watch your self-talk

Stage eight is considering what you think the affair says regarding you. The sold out life partner will frequently have negative considerations, for example, "In the event that I stay in this relationship I'm a blockhead" or "I'm detestable or probably they could not have possibly cheated." These assertions are speculations and should be changed. The unruly life partner may likewise have negative considerations about themselves, for example, "I'm a piece of junk for cheating" or "I don't merit another opportunity." our thought process decides how we feel and how we act. Accordingly, getting our contemplations straight is principal. To change your negative considerations start by thinking of them down so you can take a gander at them all the more equitably. Then, consider an elective explanation that is more adjusted and honest alongside every unique idea. For instance, in the event that the first idea is "In the event that I stay in this relationship I'm a simpleton" a changed idea could be "In the event that my accomplice hadn't removed all contact with their darling, opened all records energetically, and communicated earnest regret, I would be a dolt for remaining in this relationship. Notwithstanding, they have done those things so my choice to remain in the marriage is justified." Another model, assuming that the first idea is "I'm a piece of junk for cheating" a changed idea could be "I pursued an exceptionally unfortunate choice to swindle that was very destructive to my mate; in any case, it doesn't mean I'm a piece of rubbish. I was in an awful spot throughout everyday life and settled on a horrible choice."

Stage Nine-Fill your affection containers

Stage nine is finding the top things you want to top off your affection pail to feel cherished and fulfilled and the top things your accomplice does that depletes your adoration can. We as a whole have an adoration container within us and we as a whole need specific things to top it off. A few normal fillers incorporate love, fondness, sex, profound closeness, acts of kindness, and so on. Some normal drainers incorporate analysis, preventiveness, stalling, disdain, not sharing power, and so forth. While you're dating yourself normally top off your accomplice's affection container. Nonetheless, after you're together for a spell the vast majority quit filling their accomplice's affection container and begin depleting it all things being equal. After a short time, the full can that made you go gaga for your accomplice turns out to be increasingly more unfilled until it's dry. Dry containers increment helplessness for affairs. Hence, one of the most outstanding approaches to affair evidence your relationship pushing ahead is ensuring you're both succeeding at your accomplice's fillers they want while limiting the drainers they abhorrence to keep your pails full. Here is an article to get familiar with this model and switching a cold marriage.

Stage Ten-Foster limits

The keep going step on recuperating from an affair is examining what limits you both will follow pushing ahead to lessen your affair risk. What's that going to resemble for your relationship? For instance, how might limits look while you're voyaging away from each other? How could it look assuming you're going out with your companions for the night without your accomplice? What limits would it be advisable for you to have around partners? What might be said about at the rec center? What should your cutoff points be with liquor when you're not together? What's not satisfactory to talk about with the contrary orientation? Dealing with these inquiries is essential to foster a bound together front against future affairs. Such countless couples fall into affairs since they put themselves in hazardous circumstances without acknowledging it. Try not to allow that to happen to you. Examine what your limits as a team will be to invigorate your marriage from affairs pushing ahead.

Recovering from an affair can be a difficult and profound cycle for both partners and the accomplice who had the affair. An excursion requires persistence, responsibility, and eagerness to manage troublesome feelings and issues. The experience of recovery from an affair shifts relying upon the conditions of the affair, the characters of the people in question, and the degree of responsibility and exertion put into the recovery cycle. Here are a few normal encounters that people might experience during the recovery cycle:

Shock and mistrust: When an individual first finds that their accomplice has had an illicit relationship, they might encounter shock and doubt. They might experience issues acknowledging the situation of the circumstance and battle to deal with what has occurred.

Extreme feelings: The disclosure of an affair can set off a scope of extraordinary feelings, including outrage, hurt, disloyalty, trouble, and disarray. These feelings can be overpowering and may get some margin to process.

Self-question: The sold out accomplice might encounter self-uncertainty and question their self-esteem, appeal, and worth in the relationship.

Reconstructing trust: Remaking trust is a basic part of recuperating from an affair. A progressive cycle requires reliable exertion and open correspondence from the two accomplices.

Looking for help: Recuperating from an affair can be a desolate and disconnecting experience. Looking for help from companions, family, or a specialist can be useful in exploring the profound high points and low points of the recovery cycle.

Pardoning: Absolution is a basic part of the recovery cycle, yet it very well may be a troublesome and complex feeling to explore. Pardoning doesn't mean neglecting or overlooking the way of behaving, but instead an eagerness to relinquish outrage and disdain and push ahead.

Pushing ahead: Recuperating from an affair is difficult, yet with time and exertion, it is feasible to push ahead and construct a more grounded, better relationship. It requires a guarantee to the recovery cycle, a readiness to convey straightforwardly and truly, and a promise to building trust and closeness in the relationship.

Generally, recuperating from an affair is a complicated and close to home interaction that requires responsibility, persistence, and eagerness to deal with troublesome feelings and issues. With time, exertion, and the help of friends and family, it is feasible to push ahead and fabricate a more grounded, better relationship.

Chapter 1

Finding Your Way Back to Each Other

The repair process

When a relationship is broken, it can seem like the world is crashing down. You may feel lost, confused, and unsure of how to move forward. When trust in a relationship, it can shake the very foundation of the bond between two people. Trust is a good aspect of any relationship, and when it is breached, it can be an extremely painful and distressing experience. At first, the shock and disbelief may make you question whether the betrayal actually occurred or whether it was just a misunderstanding. As the reality sets in, the emotions may become overwhelming and intense, such as anger, sadness, hurt, and confusion. You may feel like you've been let down or that your partner has failed you in a significant way. The emotional pain can take a toll on your physical health as well. You may experience physical symptoms such as loss of appetite, difficulty sleeping, and a general sense of unease or anxiety. You may feel like you are constantly on edge, waiting for more bad news to come. As time goes on, the effects of the broken trust can become more complex. You may begin to question your own judgment and feel insecure. You may wonder if you missed warning signs that could have alerted you to the betrayal. You may also start to feel like you are not good enough or that you somehow deserve to be treated poorly. The scars left by the broken trust can last a lifetime and make it challenging to trust others in the future, even if they have done nothing wrong. It can also lead to a loss of intimacy and closeness in the relationship, as well as a breakdown in communication and mutual understanding. However, healing is possible. To start the healing process, it's crucial to acknowledge the betrayal and your feelings surrounding it. Communication is key, and it's essential to express your emotions and concerns to your partner. This can help you both understand the underlying issues and work together to rebuild trust. Recovering affair requires consistency and transparency. It's important for your partner to acknowledge the hurt they caused and take responsibility for their actions. They should be willing to answer your questions openly and honestly and take steps to regain your trust. It's also essential to establish healthy boundaries and expectations to prevent future breaches of trust.

Broken trust in a relationship can be a devastating experience, but it is possible to heal and move forward. The process takes time, effort, and a willingness to be vulnerable and open, but with consistent effort, it's possible to regain trust and build a stronger, more resilient relationship. But with time, healing, and a willingness to work on things, it is possible to find your way back to each other and repair a broken relationship. The first step in the repair process is acknowledging the issues that led to the breakup. It's good to take responsibility for your own actions and reflect on how your behavior may have contributed to the problems in the relationship. This self-reflection can be difficult, but it's necessary in order to move forward and make positive changes. Once you've identified the issues, it's important to communicate openly and honestly with your ex-partner. This can be a difficult situation to have, but it's important to be vulnerable and honest about your feelings and desires for the future of the relationship. This conversation should be done in a calm and respectful manner, without blame or criticism. If your ex-partner is willing to work on the relationship, it's important to set clear and realistic goals for the future. This can include establishing healthy communication habits, making time for each other, and being willing to compromise and make sacrifices for the relationship. These goals should be discussed openly and revisited regularly to ensure that both partners are on the same page. In addition to setting goals, it's important to take action to show your commitment to the relationship. This can include making time for each other, going on dates, and engaging in activities that you both enjoy. These actions can help to rebuild trust and create positive memories in the relationship. Along with taking action, it's important to be patient and understanding during the repair process. It's unlikely that the relationship will be fixed overnight, and there may be setbacks and challenges along the way. But with patience and a willingness to work through these difficulties together, it is possible to find your way back to each other and repair a broken relationship. Ultimately, the repair process requires a willingness to change and a commitment to the relationship. It's important to be open and honest about your feelings and desires and to work together to establish clear goals for the future. With time, patience, and a willingness to work through difficulties, it is possible to find your way back to each other and create a stronger, healthier relationship. It's important to remember that repairing a broken relationship is not an easy or quick process. It requires time, effort, and patience from both parties involved. It's also good to acknowledge that not all relationships can or should be repaired and that it's okay to let go if the relationship is toxic or unhealthy.

Assuming both parties are willing to work on repairing the relationship, here are some steps to consider:

1. Acknowledge and take responsibility for your part in the break. This requires honesty and introspection. What behaviors or actions did you engage in that contributed to the break? This is not about blame or shame but about taking ownership of your actions and their impact on the relationship.

2. Communicate openly and honestly. This means expressing your thoughts, feelings and needs in a respectful and non-blaming way and being willing tolisten to the other person's perspective. This can be challenging, especially if there is a history of communication breakdowns, but it's crucial for Recovering affair and connection.

3. Set boundaries and expectations. Once you've had an open and honest conversation, it's important to establish clear boundaries and expectations for moving forward. This could include things like agreeing to take things slow, committing to regular check-ins or counseling, or agreeing to certain behaviors or actions that will help rebuild trust.

4. Practice forgiveness. Forgiveness is not about forgetting hurtful behavior but about releasing negative emotions and moving forward. This can be difficult, especially if there has been deep betrayal or hurt, but it's essential for repairing the relationship.

5. Take action to rebuild trust. This could include things like being consistent in your actions, following through on commitments, and being transparent about your thoughts and feelings. Trust is built through consistent and reliable behavior over time.

6. Seek outside help if needed. Sometimes, despite our best efforts, we need outside help to repair a relationship. This could include couples therapy, individual therapy, or mediation.

Negative Cycles

Couples often get involved in "negative cycles," a pattern of interaction that causes problems within a marriage. The cycle begins as an initial reaction to a partner's behavior and escalates from there. Understanding and processing maladaptive interactions is a first step in preventing future problems. The following exercise will help illustrate how you relate to your partner to inform positive change.

1: Describe a repeating behavior that your partner exhibits that frequently triggers a negative cycle (e.g., my partner makes a negative comment about my family):

_____

_____

2: After I am triggered, I often react by (e.g., I curse at my partner):

_____

_____

3: My partner often reacts to me by (e.g., My partner shuts down):

_____

_____

4: When my partner reacts this way, I often feel (e.g., like they do not care):

_____

_____

5: When I react the way I do, I guess that my partner feels (e.g., like I am needy):

_____

_____

Reassurance Tips

Recovering affair after it has been broken in a relationship can be a difficult and painful process. It is possible to repair the damage and move forward. Here are some reassurance tips to help repair broken trust with your partner:

Acknowledge the hurt and take responsibility

The key to repairing trust is to acknowledge the hurt that has been caused and take responsibility for your actions. It's important to listen to your partner and their feelings and to avoid minimizing or dismissing their pain. Take responsibility for your behavior and show that you are committed to changing it.

Be transparent and open

Transparency and open communication are key to rebuilding trust. Be willing to share your thoughts, feelings, and actions with your partner, and avoid keeping secrets or withholding information. Being open and transparent can help to demonstrate your commitment to the relationship and to rebuilding trust.

Follow through on promises

If you make a promise to your partner, make sure that you follow through on it. This can help to demonstrate your commitment to the relationship and to rebuilding trust. Be reliable and show that you can be counted on.

Show empathy and understanding

Demonstrating empathy and understanding can help to rebuild trust by showing your partner that you care about their feelings and are willing to see things from their perspective. Listen actively, validate their feelings, and show that you are committed to making things right.

Take steps to prevent future breaches of trust

In order to rebuild trust, it's important to take steps to prevent future breaches of trust. This might involve setting clear boundaries, agreeing on expectations, or seeking help from a therapist or counselor. By taking proactive steps to prevent future problems, you can demonstrate your commitment to the relationship and to rebuilding trust.

Be patient and consistent

Recovering affair is a process that takes time, effort, and patience. It's important to be consistent in your behavior and actions and to avoid becoming defensive or impatient. Be willing to put in the effort needed to repair the damage, and be patient as your partner works through their feelings.

Seek professional help

Sometimes, repairing broken trust requires the help of a professional. A therapist can give a safe and supportive environment for you and your partner to work through your issues and rebuild trust. They can provide guidance and support and help you to develop strategies to strengthen your relationship.

Practice forgiveness

It can help to release the anger and resentment that can build up after trust has been broken and allow you to move forward. Forgiveness doesn't mean forgetting or excusing the behavior but rather choosing to let go of the negative emotions and focusing on moving forward.

Take care of yourself

Recovering affair can be a difficult and emotional process, and it's important to take care of yourself during this time. Make time for activities, such as exercise, meditation, or spending time with supportive friends. Take care of your emotional health, and be kind to yourself as you work through the challenges of rebuilding trust.

Repairing broken trust in a relationship is not an easy process, but it is possible. By taking responsibility for your actions, being transparent and open, following through on promises, showing empathy and understanding, taking steps to prevent future breaches of trust, being patient and consistent, seeking professional help if necessary, practicing forgiveness, and taking care of yourself, you can begin to rebuild trust and strengthen your relationship. Remember that trust takes time to build and can be easily broken, but with effort and commitment, it is possible to regain it.

Partner Appreciation

One of the most important aspects of maintaining a satisfying romantic relationship is appreciation. Unfortunately, expressing appreciation towards a partner may be lacking or wane over time. Fill out this worksheet on your own and then share with your partner during a couples therapy session. Try to find at least five answers for each question.

My partner shows me they care by:
1 _____
2 _____
3 _____
4 _____
5 _____

My favorite memories with my partner are:
1 _____
2 _____
3 _____
4 _____
5 _____

The qualities that attracted me to my partner were:
1 _____
2 _____
3 _____
4 _____
5 _____

I appreciate my partner because:
1 _____
2 _____
3 _____
4 _____
5 _____

Establishing a safe space

Establishing a safe space in a relationship is crucial for building trust and maintaining a healthy partnership. A safe space is an environment where both partners feel comfortable sharing their thoughts, feelings, and vulnerabilities without fear of judgment or rejection.

Creating a safe space requires intentional effort and a willingness to prioritize the emotional well-being of your partner. Here are tips to establish a safe space in your relationship:

1. Communicate openly and honestly: Communication is key in any relationship, and it is especially important when establishing a safe space. Be open about your feelings and thoughts. Encourage them to do the same and listen actively without interrupting or judging. Try to avoid being defensive or dismissive of their concerns.

2. Practice active listening: Active listening is a component of creating a safe space. It involves focusing on what your partner is saying, understanding their perspective, and responding in a way that you understand them. This means avoiding distractions, such as your phone or TV, and giving your partner your full attention.

3. Be empathetic: Empathy is the ability to share the feelings of another person. It is an important skill in creating a safe space. Try to understand how they are feeling. Let them know that you have a concern about their feelings and that you are there to support them.

4. Avoid judgment and criticism: Judging and criticizing your partner can make them feel defensive and less likely to open up. Instead, try to approach conversations with an open mind and avoid attacking or belittling your partner's thoughts or feelings.

5. Set boundaries: Setting boundaries is an important aspect of creating a safe space. It involves being clear about what behaviors are and are not acceptable in the relationship. This can include things like respecting each other's privacy, not

yelling or using abusive language, and taking responsibility for your own actions.

6. Build on your strengths: Focusing on the positive aspects of your relationship can help create a safe space. Take time to acknowledge the things you appreciate about each other and build on those strengths. This can help create a more positive and supportive environment.

Establishing a safe space in a relationship is essential for building trust and maintaining a healthy partnership. By communicating honestly, practicing active listening, being empathetic, avoiding judgment and criticism, practicing forgiveness, setting boundaries, and building on your strengths, you can create a safe and supportive environment for both you and your partner.

SAFE SPACES
for EVERYONE

Getting to know your Partner

Although you might find it surprising, many couples don't know their partners that well. Having knowledge of your partner I a key to emotional intimacy, one of the most important factors in a good relationship. The following questions help assess how well a couple knows each other and what areas may need to be further addressed. These questions can be asked by a partner during a couples therapy session or for an assignment at home.

1. What stressors are facing right now? _____

2. Describe what I did yesterday. _____

3. What is one of my greatest fears? _____

4. What is my favorite time of day? _____

5. What turns me on sexually? _____

6. What is my favorite color? _____

7. What personal improvements do I
    want to make in my life? _____

8. What is one of my favorite ways to
    be soothed? _____

9. Who is my greatest source of support? _____

10. What is my favorite place? _____

Chapter 2

Mending the Worthy Relationship

Working on relationship

Mending a worthy relationship is crucial for many reasons, one of which is the emotional healing and closure it can provide for both partners. When trust has been broken, it can create emotional pain and turmoil that can be difficult to move past without proper communication and repair. Addressing the issues and working towards mending the relationship allows both individuals to heal from past hurts and move forward in a positive direction. A strong and healthy relationship can also lead to a more resilient partnership. When both partners are committed to rebuilding the relationship, it can strengthen the bond between them. It can create a deeper level of trust and intimacy, as both individuals have had to be vulnerable and open in order to work through their issues. This can help to build a foundation for future challenges and conflicts that may arise in the relationship.

A healthy relationship can have a positive impact on other areas of life. Having a supportive partner and a strong support system can improve overall well-being and happiness. It can provide a sense of security and stability, which can lead to greater success in other areas of life, such as work or personal goals. The positive effects of a healthy relationship can extend beyond the couple themselves and into their families and communities as well. Mending a worthy relationship is important because it can serve as a model for other relationships in our lives. When we work through our issues and create a strong and healthy relationship, it can inspire others to do the same. We become an example for others to follow and can help to create a ripple effect of healthy relationships and positive communication in our social circles. It's also important to note that mending a relationship doesn't mean that the problems or issues will disappear completely. Rather, it means that both partners are willing to work together to find solutions and move forward in a positive direction. It requires ongoing effort and communication to maintain a healthy relationship. However, the benefits of mending a worthy relationship are well worth the effort and can lead to a happier and more fulfilling life for both individuals involved.

Sophie and Tom sat on the couch, looking at each other with tense expressions. They had been arguing about Tom's lack of communication and trust in their relationship for weeks, and it seemed like they were at an impasse. Finally, Sophie spoke up.

Sophie: "Tom, I know we've been struggling lately, but I really believe that we have a worthy relationship that's worth fighting for."

Tom: "I know, Sophie. I want to make terms right between us, but I just don't know how to fix things."

Sophie: "I think the first step is to establish a safe space where we can be honest and vulnerable with each other. We need to talk about our feelings without fear of judgment or anger."

Tom: "That sounds good, but how do we do that?"

Sophie: "We start by listening to each other without interrupting or getting defensive. We need to acknowledge each other's feelings, even if we don't agree with them. And most importantly, we need to show empathy and compassion towards each other."

Tom: "I think I can do that. It's just hard to let my guard down after all that's happened."

Sophie: "I understand, Tom. But we need to take a leap of faith if we want to mend our relationship. It won't happen overnight, but if we commit to working on things together, I truly believe we can go back."

Tom: "I want to try, Sophie. I don't want to lose you."

Sophie: "I love you too, Tom. Let's make this work."

With that, Sophie and Tom embraced and began the journey of mending their worthy relationship. It wasn't easy, but they committed to creating a safe space where they could communicate openly and honestly with each other. Over time, their bond grew stronger, and they were able to overcome the trust issues that had been plaguing their relationship. They knew that they still had work to do, but they were grateful for the love and support they found in each other.

Write Your Feelings If you were Sophie or Tom in the Story

When you lay down with somebody you're laying down with every individual they've laid down with. I don't have any idea how far back to take this. Does it imply that I've potentially laid down with Abraham Lincoln and Henry the Eighth? Be that as it may, I get the point. What's more, similarly, it's likewise a fact that when you engage with somebody you need to manage every one of the double-crossings they've encountered from everybody they were engaged with before you. You might in all likelihood never have sold out anybody yourself. Yet, some way or another you are ensnared in treachery in any case. In the event that a person starts dating a lady whose past beau used to beat her, that new person must manage the lady's feeling of dread toward his beating her. This can feel awfully unreasonable. Be that as it may, it's exceptionally considered normal, more so today than any time in recent memory. Individuals are getting hitched later than previously, having been in additional connections before they wed. Individuals we wed have not exclusively been there, done that a lot of times, they've gotten run north of a couple of times, as well. Simply consider it. When the typical young lady, for instance, is eighteen she's had her heart broken no less than once by a few kid and has been horrendously sold out by one of her companions. There's no counting the number of stories that she's found out about comparative encounters. She's most presumably survived a separation, whether her folks' or that of a family member or a dear companion's folks. What's more, it's essentially no different for men. I know this since I've asked people when they previously discovered that trust would have been a pain point in their lives. It generally starts at eighteen or prior. Furthermore, assuming that it resembles at eighteen, envision what this resembles when individuals are 28 and afterward 38 and afterward 48, etc. With each year we aggregate more personal information on every one of the manners in which individuals let each other down. Perhaps we've done a portion of the letting down ourselves. let each other down. Perhaps we've done a portion of the letting down ourselves. Ponder how this treats us.

At any point Only this previous year, Tracy, a lady in her forties, sat opposite me and asked me with the most piercing maxim, "Answer this inquiry — and whether I commit suicide relies upon your response: Can I trust a man once more?" Tracy was separated. Her ex had deceived her by not being the man she thought he was. He'd ended up being self-centered and basic rather than liberal and steady. Then, at that point, she'd experienced passionate feelings for a man … indeed, "love" isn't exactly the word for it. It was, as per her, a relationship of stupendous profundity and closeness and enthusiasm. They felt, she expressed, associated as no two individuals had at any point been associated. That they would share their lives and prospects appeared to be incontestable. And afterward he unloaded her. A surprise out of nowhere in the event that there at any point was one, sending her into a self-destructive melancholy. Her inquiry to me, miserable as it was, and setting to the side the danger of self-destruction, seemed OK. How might she at any point trust a man once more?

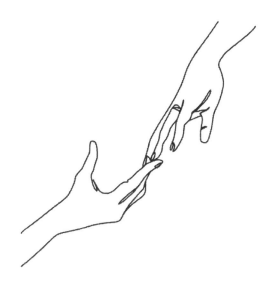

An Alternate point of view. We should check out at this according to an alternate point of view briefly. Assume Tracy one day chose to take one more risk on adoration. What how about it seem like to be that new person? It could be unpleasant, wouldn't you say? I'm certain Tracy will do what everybody in her circumstance does: avoid the individual she engages with next as much as possible until she trusts him, then again, actually she never will trust him. She'll continuously be watching for the unavoidable conclusion. Burnt out on hanging tight for a sensation of trust that never comes, she'll need to speed up the cycle. In the event that she can some way or another put him under serious scrutiny, then, at that point, perhaps she'll feel more secure. So she'll do to him how producers manage a piece of gear that should be utilized in an exceptionally substantial climate. She'll put him through each challenge she can imagine. And afterward what might occur? You and I both know the response. On the off chance that he enjoys adequately her, he'll hold tight while she drags him through hellfire, being pretty much as troublesome as could be expected. She'll fly off the handle with him over seemingly insignificant details. She'll be flighty. She'll be far off. She'll be a modest bunch. Yet, eventually he will become ill of the troubles and sever things. And afterward she'll feel approved that to be sure you can't trust any person. that for sure you can't trust any person. It can likewise work out in a totally different manner. Rather than holding him at a manageable distance, she can hold herself at a manageable distance. Rather than being troublesome, she can simply not be there. Certainly, they'll make an insincere effort as may be obvious. As may be obvious, it's a typical, creating relationship. Yet, what nobody can see, perhaps not even Tracy herself, is that she's set her heart aside momentarily. This might appear to be an entirely exquisite relationship, she shares with herself, however I can't trust it any farther than I can toss it, so I'll come as though this relationship were occurring to another person. This is a safe yet terrible technique. It's protected on the grounds that you're resistant from getting injured. It's awful on the grounds that you can never feel any of the great stuff while you're keeping your heart secured in its own confidential cooler.

The most widely recognized design these days is a blend of these two different ways for things to work out. The vast majority of us could do without to introduce ourselves as casualties of treachery when we're simply getting to know somebody. On the initial not many dates, most likely neither of you will haul out your accounts of the manners in which you've been deceived. What's more, regardless of whether you, you'll presumably delicate pedal your fury and mistrust. This implies that the two individuals are powerless. I, with my mistrust, am defenseless against being wounded by you. But at the same time you're helpless against being wounded by me assuming you guiltlessly accomplish something that in some way animates my mistrust. This is a significant gamble factor for our having the option to get together. No big surprise there is a far off or thorny quality to such countless connections. Individuals aren't treading lightly. They're strolling on the dry, weak bones of past disloyalties. This is the heart-on-ice stage. Then sooner or later, all of a sudden, comes the stage where you move out of the wardrobe and check whether the other individual can deal with the genuine you. Presently you can perceive how the manners in which we've been harmed in past connections can make a major wreck in our ongoing one. Arrangements

How on earth do you manage this? How might you at any point track down both security and love in the event that you or your partner has been harmed previously?

Yet, imagine a scenario where you're engaged with somebody who's been harmed before. You must be obviously genuine with yourself. Assuming you're with somebody who in the past was harmed more than most, you may be in for some extreme sledding. This won't be a support free relationship. Regardless of whether the other individual has paid attention to my recommendation not to put you through an experience, there's actually going to be a portion of that. Also there will be less edge for blunder when you screw up. What's more, we as a whole screw up. So you need to inquire as to whether the other individual is worth the effort. Do that now before you get in any more profound. What's more, in the event that you understand it's not worth the effort, go ahead and. Individuals frequently commit a tremendous and horrendous error here. They're with somebody who's been harmed, thus they would rather not hurt them any longer. So they remain despite the fact that they need to leave. This simply compounds the situation. The unavoidable separation will occur; it's simply that presently you'll go through months or long periods of the other individual's life and harmed them significantly more. Assuming you conclude that the other individual is worth the effort — indeed, he's been seriously harmed previously, however he's smart, normal, beguiling, and alluring — here are a few standards to keep that will mend the other individual's mistrust. Coincidentally: You ought to observe these guidelines at whatever point you're in a circumstance where you need to procure the other individual's trust. Try not to screw up. Indeed, I know, you're somewhat flawed. Nobody anticipates that you should be. Be that as it may, ponder this similarity: Assume you went to an eatery and tracked down a bug in your plate of mixed greens. Yowser! You caused an uproar and the board was extremely sorry and didn't charge you for your dinner. Then, at that point, suppose you chose to allow them another opportunity and return two or after three weeks. Couldn't you want to believe that they could remember you and put forth an additional attempt to ensure that nothing turns out badly? All things considered, for what reason would it be advisable for it be any unique for individuals in our lives. They realize that you realize that they've been harmed. So they simply believe you should make an additional that you realize that they've been harmed. So they simply believe you should put forth an additional attempt not to hurt them once more. What sorts of things am I referring to? Nothing all that surprising. Just things like not failing to remember the individual's birthday. Not returning home late without a fair warning. Not expressing mean things. Not looking at different ladies when you're out with her. Also, remember to ask how you might show that you care about not harming her. This isn't tied in with being great. We as a whole commit errors. Along these lines, OK, commit your portion of errors. Be that as it may, to acquire somebody's trust, particularly when she's been harmed previously, try not to commit the huge errors.

Try not to lie or be covered up. I've seen something exceptionally fascinating: Individuals who've been harmed in past connections frequently imagine that the individual they're with now is a liar. Why would that be? Is it maybe suspicion? No. I accept that individuals who've been harmed in past connections are bound to be deceived by their ongoing partner. Also, here's the reason. On the off chance that you're involved with somebody who's been harmed a great deal, she will be entirely helpless. Yet, you, similar to every other person, are exceptionally flawed. Furthermore, what do you think happens when Mr. Defective meets Ms. Defenseless? Blasts will follow. One of the apparently most effective ways to safeguard the individual who's been harmed a ton is to lie and stow away. The allurement is practically overpowering. On the off chance that you can keep something terrible from her, she will not get injured! Now and again, this strategy of lying and concealing works. It works just frequently to the point of keeping us making it happen. What's more, that is the reason individuals who've been harmed turn out to be misled. In any case, this is a horrible strategy, definitely more damaging over the long haul than the other option. That is on the grounds that reality quite often emerges. Furthermore, for somebody who's been harmed, being misled or deluded is far more awful than nearly whatever else. So regardless of whether it could cause you some distress in the short run, be basically as legit and open as could be expected. Each and every piece of concealment, embellishment, or twisting will take care of the monster. You need to starve the monster to death. You comprehend that you will get some melancholy for your genuineness in the short run. Nobody enjoys the unlucky messenger. So you have a little contention. What of it? Your continuously being transparent will make you a trusted individual over the long haul and your partner will feel a lot more secure. Try not to make guarantees you won't keep. We as a whole succumb to this. We feel we're being compelled by somebody and we need to get him away from us. So we make a commitment. "Fine, I'll clear out the storeroom this end of the week." Or, "Fine, I'll converse with my supervisor about that raise." We might have good motivations, however when we're out of that snapshot of tension, the commitment out of nowhere appears to be to a lesser degree a smart thought. Or on the other hand it ends up being less feasible. So you don't keep the commitment, and you trust that the other individual won't notice or will acknowledge your reason. Obviously, generally the circumstance adopts a totally different strategy. The fact that you've broken a commitment makes him staggered and harmed. He feels deceived. Furthermore, obviously, you before long get into a major battle where the other individual attempts to show why this is a tremendous, serious deal and you attempt to show them for what reason they're insane not to believe it's a little arrangement. These battles seldom end well. So while you're managing somebody who is at all delicate — and truly, we are in general delicate with regards to feeling deceived — simply do this. Never under any circumstance, make a commitment except if you totally realize that you will keep it. Continuously stay conservative then shock everyone with something amazing. Watch out. You may properly feel that the other individual is beseeching you to give them an assurance that you will follow through with something. All aspects of you might feel that you simply need to get this individual away from you. It doesn't make any difference. Try not to guarantee what you will not convey.

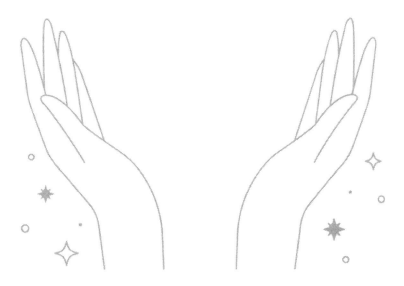

Acceptance

Aspects of my partner that I find hard to accept	Aspects of myself that I find hard to accept
Aspects of my partner that I am still learning to accept	Aspects of myself that I am still learning to accept
Aspects of my partner that I have come to accept	Aspects of myself that I have come to accept
Aspects of my partner that I like, value and/or respect	Aspects of myself that I like, value and/or respect

Approve; don't go against

Here is an almost widespread mistake, and it's extremely horrendous. Your partner blasts forward with some apprehension or complaint including you. You feel under attack. So you do with your partner how you would likely not manage your companion: You give her a contention. You attempt to persuade her that she's off-base for feeling the manner in which she feels. Furthermore, what does that achieve? All it does is cause her to feel that you simply don't get it, and she feels significantly more helpless. Assume she discusses how she's worried you will undermine her the manner in which her ex did. Assuming you manage her trepidation by saying, "That is senseless. I could never undermine you," she's about to feel you've excused her. Which is, obviously, what a miscreant would do? All things considered, you really want to express something like, "I comprehend. Folks have undermined you previously. Also, there I'm out working the entire day however you don't have the foggiest idea where I and I'm doing. I thoroughly get it that you're worried about the possibility that that I may be cheating and you wouldn't be aware." Then ask her how you might console her. Let her tell you. I know that feels like you were giving her ammo. However, approval like this will constantly attempt to modify trust. A hurt individual's feelings of dread aren't something to be brushed away with a flyswatter. All things considered, they're a chance for you to show that you treat the other individual's requirements in a serious way. Certain individuals are hesitant to do this since they believe that approving the other individual implies that you're concurring with their unreasonable feelings of dread. Yet, you're not concurring with their unreasonable feelings of trepidation by any means. You're not, for instance, saying, "OK, you're correct, I will undermine you." No, you're simply saying, "I comprehend that you feel as such, and I grasp the reason why." Acknowledge that the other individual doesn't have a solid sense of security. The enticement is practically overpowering. Sooner or later you will want to shout, "Stop it! I'm not Ann, Mary, Isabel, or any of different young ladies who hurt you. I'm me and I won't hurt you. So cut it out." However enticing as this may be, it's a misstep. The other individual will ultimately feel more secure yet it can happen when he's prepared. Assuming you advise him to stop before he's prepared he's about to hear that you don't believe he should be how he is. Acknowledge the way that part of the value of being with this individual is the means by which simple it will be for him to feel perilous when something comes up that invigorates his doubt. Think about it along these lines. At the point when you're with somebody who's been harmed previously, you have the (presumably) long lasting errand of being there for him as he is. It would be ideal to imagine that you won't ever harm him, yet it's difficult to totally try not to hurt somebody you care about. On the off chance that you can show that you're there for him and that implies tolerating him how he is, then you've done everything an individual can manage.

Theory A and Theory B: for couples

Theory A: "one of us is the problem and should change"	Theory B: "we have a problem and we need to change"
How is one of us the problem? Partner A Partner B	How are we the problem – what's our vicious cycle?
What is the evidence for Theory A? Partner A Partner B	What is the evidence for Theory B?
What should we do if Theory A is true?	What should we do if Theory B is true?

Is It Worth It?

Working on a relationship can be a challenging process, but it can be incredibly rewarding and worthwhile. Whether a relationship is worth working on ultimately depends on the individuals involved and the level of commitment and effort they are willing to put in. If both partners are committed to the relationship and are willing to put in the work to repair any issues or conflicts, then it can be worth it. This may involve seeking help, such as couples therapy or counseling, in order to work through difficult issues and improve communication. However, if one or both partners are not willing to put in the effort to repair the relationship or are unwilling to make necessary changes, then it may not be worth continuing. It is important to assess whether the relationship is healthy and fulfilling for both individuals and to be honest with oneself about whether the effort required to work on the relationship is worth it in the long run. Ultimately, the decision to work on a relationship should be made based on individual values and priorities. If a strong and healthy relationship is a priority, then it may be worth investing time and effort to work through any issues. However, if the relationship is causing significant emotional pain or is not fulfilling, then it may be time to reassess and consider moving on. It is important to remember that working on a relationship is not a one-time event but rather an ongoing process. It requires commitment, communication, and a willingness to make necessary changes in order to build a strong and healthy partnership.

Individual differences	Assets/strengths: complementary roles, division of tasks	
	I am good at…	You are good at…
	Deficits/weaknesses: vulnerability to change	
	I am not so good at…	You are not so good at…

Couple similarities	Assets/strengths: symmetrical roles, shared tasks
	Both of us are good at…
	Deficits/weaknesses: need for support or personal development
	Neither of us is so good at…

Why not give it a Try?

When a relationship is broken, it can be tempting to simply give up and move on. But before throwing in the towel, it's important to consider whether it's worth working on establishing the relationship. While it may require a great deal of effort, time, and patience, there are many reasons why trying to repair a broken relationship is often the best course of action. One of the primary reasons to work on establishing a broken relationship is that it can provide a sense of closure and allow people to move forward in a positive direction. If there are unresolved issues or lingering hurt feelings, it can be difficult to let go of the past and move on. By working to address these issues and repair the relationship, it can provide a sense of closure and allow both individuals to move forward in a positive way. Additionally, working on establishing a broken relationship can lead to a stronger and more resilient partnership. When both individuals are committed to repairing the relationship and are willing to put in the effort, it can strengthen the bond between them. As Dr. Gary Chapman, author of "The 5 Love Languages," notes, "Love is something you do for someone else, not something you do for yourself. It is not based on the merit or worthiness of the recipient, but on the choice of the giver."

It's good to remember that relationships are not always easy. As human beings, we have flaws, insecurities, and shortcomings. But if we are willing to work through these issues and support one another, we can build a stronger and more loving partnership. As author Leo Buscaglia once said, "A loving relationship is the loved one is free to be himself to cry with me, but never because of me; to love the life, to love himself, to love being loved. Such a relationship is based on freedom and can never grow in a jealous heart." Of course, working on establishing a broken relationship is not always easy. It can be painful, frustrating, and challenging. By putting in the effort to repair the relationship, both parties can reap the benefits of a stronger and more loving partnership.

So why not give it a try? As author and relationship expert Dr. John Gottman notes, "When couples do the work to repair a broken relationship, it can bring them closer together than they were before." By taking the time to work through the issues, communicate openly and honestly, and support one another, it's possible to establish a relationship that is stronger, more resilient, and more loving than ever before. In order to work on establishing a broken relationship, there are several steps that can be taken. The first step is to talk openly and honestly with one another. This means being willing to listen to one another's perspectives and feelings without judgment or defensiveness. As relationship expert Esther Perel notes, "The quality of your all the relationships determines the quality of your life."

Another important step is to be willing to make changes and compromises in order to repair the relationship. This may mean letting go of past hurts or resentments, being more supportive and understanding of one another's needs and wants, and making an effort to be more present and engaged in the relationship.

Finally, it's important to seek outside support if necessary. This may mean getting help from someone who can provide guidance and support as both individuals work to repair the relationship. By taking the time and effort to work on repairing a broken relationship, both individuals have the opportunity to heal and grow together. This can lead to a deeper level of trust, understanding, and intimacy, as well as a stronger and more resilient partnership.

Therefore, it is worth putting in the effort to repair a broken relationship, as it can have positive effects on all areas of our lives. In addition, author Mandy Hale reminds us that "Sometimes two people have to fall to realize how much they should need to fall back both together." By going through the process of repairing a broken relationship, both individuals may come to a greater appreciation of each other and their relationship.

It's important to remember that repairing a broken relationship is not always easy or quick. It takes time and a willingness to be vulnerable and open with your partner. As relationship coach Jayson Gaddis notes, "Fixing a relationship is like gardening. You don't plant the seed and then come back the next day expecting a full-grown plant. It takes time, attention, and patience." However, the rewards of a strong and healthy relationship can be worth the effort. As author Shannon L. Alder states, "Relationships are like gardens. They are constantly changing and growing. They need to be nurtured, weeded, and sometimes pruned in order to flourish." By putting in the effort to repair a broken relationship, both individuals have the opportunity to nurture and grow their partnership into something beautiful and fulfilling. Ultimately, working on establishing a broken relationship is often worth it. As author and relationship expert Dr. Sue Johnson notes, "When couples are willing to put in the time and effort to repair a broken relationship, it can lead to a deeper sense of love, intimacy, and connection.

Improving my relationship by being the best partner I can be

For the good of the relationship and for the sake of my partner and others that I love;

For my own well>being and integrity, I will strive to be the best partner I can be

Task one: facing up to myself

Write down all the things about your current behaviour as a partner that could be unsatisfactory, hurtful and/or wrong:

_____

_____

_____

Task two: improving my actions

Write down all the things that you would like to see yourself doing if your relationship were all that it could be:

_____

_____

_____

Task three: problem>solving

Identify all the helpful strategies that you could use to tackle these obstacles:

_____

_____

_____

Task four:

Combine tasks three and four by writing down your intentions in the form 'If (obstacle occurs) then (strategy I will use)' E.g. "If I forget to tell my partner I am grateful for their help on an important project then I will buy them a thank you card in my next lunch hour" or "If I don't feel like doing a job I have said I will do at the time I agreed to do it then I will remind myself why this is important to my partner, to the relationship and to me":

_____

_____

_____

Chapter 3

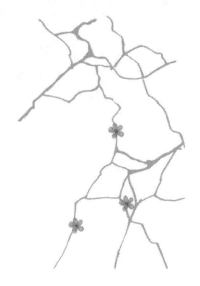

Success Stories of Relationships after Facing Mistrust

When trust gets broken in a relationship, it can feel like an insurmountable challenge to try and repair the damage. However, success stories abound of couples who have managed to work through their issues and rebuild the trust that was lost.

Sarah and James

One such couple is Sarah and James, who had been together for several years when Sarah discovered James had been unfaithful. Despite the initial devastation and uncertainty, they were able to work through their issues and rebuild their relationship. Sarah says, "It was a long road, but we were both committed to working on our relationship and rebuilding trust. It wasn't an easy task, but it was worth it. We're now stronger and closer than ever before."

Mark and Emily

Mark and Emily's story is another success story. When Mark lied about something important, it caused a rift in their relationship, and Emily felt hurt and couldn't trust him anymore. But with open communication and counseling, they were able to work through their issues and regain trust. Mark says, "It was a wake-up call for me. I realized that my actions had consequences and that I needed to work hard to regain Emily's trust. We both put in the effort, and now our relationship is stronger than ever."

Rebecca Story

Rebecca was a successful lawyer who had been married to her husband, Daniel, a musician and composer. Despite their busy schedules, they had a great relationship and shared a passion for nature, music, and Latin dancing. However, everything changed when Rebecca caught Daniel cheating on her with a young woman he was giving guitar lessons to. Devastated by the betrayal, Rebecca turned to a relationship expert for help. The expert urged Rebecca to bring Daniel to their next session, and it was there that they discovered Daniel's naivety and heartbreak. He had no idea how badly Rebecca would react to his infidelity and was shocked to learn that she saw it as the murder of a loved one. Despite the hurt and betrayal, the couple started to rebuild the trust that had been broken. They talked openly and honestly about what had happened, and Daniel vowed to fight for their marriage. However, Rebecca still felt stuck, unsure if she could ever trust him again. Then, a crazy idea came into her head. Rebecca had always wanted another child, but Daniel had been adamant about not wanting any more kids. However, if he agreed to have a child with her, not because he wanted to but because he knew it was important to her, Rebecca believed it would make a huge difference. She would know that she really mattered to him. At first, Daniel had a lot of qualms and questions, but eventually, he agreed to have a child with her. The decision was a big deal, but Rebecca believed it would help her heal faster. Years later, Rebecca and Daniel are still together, and their child is about to start kindergarten. Daniel is a wonderful dad, and their relationship is stronger than ever. Rebecca has come to trust him again, and they have both learned the importance of communication and honesty in a relationship. Despite the pain and challenges they faced, Rebecca's leap of faith paid off, and they are happier now than they ever thought possible. These success stories tell that it is possible to rebuild trust in a relationship, even after it has been broken. It takes a willingness to be vulnerable and open with your partner, but it can be done.

Cindy and Jeff

Cindy and Jeff had been married for many years, and despite their differences, they had built a strong relationship. Cindy was a successful middle-aged woman with many accomplishments under her belt. Her wild curly grey hair and peasant-style clothes made her stand out as a "Cambridge type" in Boston. Jeff, on the other hand, was a well-known writer with a worldwide reputation. He was thin, hip, and had a grizzled appearance that made him look equally at home in a West Village cocktail party or in front of a country store. But then, one day, Jeff dropped a bombshell on Cindy: he had bought a cabin on a lake in Maine where he wanted to spend time writing. It was supposed to be a personal home away from home, far from any distractions. Jeff insisted that it was not a trial separation, but Cindy couldn't help feeling hurt and betrayed. She saw it as Jeff throwing a separation at her out of nowhere. Cindy was devastated. Nothing in her world made sense anymore. She was still the same person, but now Jeff didn't want her. She couldn't look forward to going to their favorite restaurants with him anymore. She became bitter when she remembered all the good times they had shared together. "How could he throw it all away?" she wondered. Even when Jeff tries to do something nice for her, she sees it as a sign of his betrayal. She lashed out with wild machine-gun volleys of rage, trying to hit Jeff with the most wounding comments she could think of. Jeff, on the other hand, blamed the whole thing on his needing to give his writing a shot in the arm. But Cindy didn't think that was a good enough excuse. They were slowly tearing their wounded marriage apart, but they didn't know what else to do. Cindy felt like she couldn't trust someone she had loved and relied on. Jeff was in tears, asking, "What else can I say?" The pain of betrayal was like an emotional wound that wouldn't heal. Cindy felt like she had been stranded on a tiny barren desert island, and even though she could survive, it would never feel right. She lashed out because she was in so much pain. It was perfectly understandable and something that we all have done at some point in our lives. As a third-party observer, it was clear to me that Cindy and Jeff were two people who had relied on each other and loved each other. They had built a good life together, but now it seemed like it was all falling apart. It was an unbelievably sad situation, and there was no easy solution. I wished that I could help them, but the truth was, I didn't know what to say either.

Chapter 4

Recovering affair through Interactive Activities

The Cuddle Session

Trust is the base of any healthy relationship, whether it's romantic or platonic. Trust allows people to feel safe and secure with each other, knowing that they can rely on one another and that their best interests are always in mind. However, trust can also be fragile and easily broken, leading to feelings of hurt, betrayal, and a loss of connection. When trust is damaged, it takes time and effort to rebuild it. One effective way to rebuild trust is through interactive activities, such as the cuddle session.

Cuddling is an intimate act that involves holding and embracing another person. It's a physical expression of affection and can promote feelings of security, comfort, and love. Cuddling can also release oxytocin, a hormone associated with bonding and trust-building. The cuddle session is an interactive activity that involves intentional and focused cuddling with the purpose of rebuilding trust.

To begin a cuddle session, both parties must be willing and consenting. It's important to establish boundaries and guidelines beforehand to ensure that everyone feels safe. Communication is key during a cuddle session, and both parties should be clear about their intentions and expectations. Some ground rules for a cuddle session may include:

1. *No sexual activity*

2. *No touching of private areas*

3. *Both parties should agree to any variations in position or intensity*

4. *Either party can stop the session at any time for any reason*

Once the ground rules have been established, the cuddle session can begin. The session can take place in a comfortable and cozy environment, such as a bed or couch. Both parties should dress in comfortable clothing and have pillows and blankets nearby for added comfort.

During the cuddle session, both parties should focus on being present and attentive to each other. They should take turns holding and being held and can vary the positions and levels of intensity. The goal of the cuddle session is to promote feelings of safety, comfort, and trust and to create a space for vulnerability and emotional connection.

The cuddle session can also be used as an opportunity for verbal communication. Both parties can take turns sharing their feelings and thoughts, expressing gratitude and appreciation for each other, and acknowledging any hurt or damage that has been caused in the past. The cuddle session can be a safe and non-judgmental space for both parties to express themselves and work towards rebuilding trust.

It's important to note that the cuddle session is just one tool in the process of rebuilding trust. Trust is a complex and multifaceted concept, and it takes time and effort to rebuild after it's been damaged. The cuddle session can be a helpful activity in promoting feelings of safety, comfort, and trust, but it should be combined with other trust-building strategies, such as open communication, honesty, and consistency. Trust is vital to a healthy relationship, and it takes time and effort to build and maintain. When trust is damaged, interactive activities, such as the cuddle session, can be a helpful tool in the process of rebuilding. The cuddle session promotes feelings of safety, comfort, and trust and creates a space for vulnerability and emotional connection. However, it's important to remember that the cuddle session is just one tool in the process of Recovering affair and should be combined with other strategies to promote a healthy and trusting relationship.

Write Your Feelings

Partner 1	Partner 2

Obstacle Course

Recovering affair after a breach can be a challenging and lengthy process, requiring both time and effort from all parties involved. One useful tool for Recovering affair is the obstacle course through interactive activities. This course involves a series of activities designed to promote teamwork, communication, and mutual understanding between individuals trying to rebuild their relationships. The first step in the obstacle course is identifying the specific areas where trust has been broken. This can be achieved through open communication between the parties involved. Once these areas have been identified, the course can begin.

The obstacle course typically involves a series of physical and mental challenges that require the participants to work together in order to succeed. For example, participants might be asked to navigate a maze blindfolded or work together to solve a complex puzzle.

The purpose of these challenges is to build teamwork, communication, and trust between the participants. By working together to overcome these obstacles, individuals can learn to trust one another again and develop a sense of shared purpose. Another important aspect of the obstacle course is the element of risk-taking. In order to rebuild trust, individuals must be willing to take risks and put themselves in vulnerable positions. This can be difficult, as trust has been broken, and individuals may be hesitant to open up again. However, by working through the obstacles together, participants can build a sense of safety and security with one another. The obstacle course can also involve opportunities for reflection and feedback. After completing each challenge, participants can discuss their experiences and offer feedback to one another. This provides an opportunity for individuals to express their thoughts and feelings in a safe and supportive environment. Overall, the obstacle course through interactive activities is a powerful tool for rebuilding trust. By promoting teamwork, communication, and risk-taking, individuals can learn to trust one another again and develop a stronger sense of shared purpose.

Worksheet

This worksheet is designed to guide couples through an obstacle course activity that is aimed at recovering affair and improving communication in their relationship.

Instructions:

1. *Set up an obstacle course: Create a physical obstacle course in a safe and open space that both you and your partner can navigate. Use various obstacles such as cones, hurdles, ropes, balance beams, etc.*

2. *Assign roles: One partner will be the "guide" and the other will be the "blindfolded" participant.*

3. *Establish rules: Set up rules for the activity. For example, no running or rushing, clear communication is essential, and safety is a priority.*

4. *Begin the activity: The "blindfolded" participant will be guided through the obstacle course by the "guide" partner. The "guide" partner will give clear and concise instructions, such as "step over the hurdle with your left foot" or "turn right at the cone ahead." The "blindfolded" participant must trust their partner to guide them safely through the course.*

5. *Switch roles: After completing the course, switch roles and repeat the activity.*

6. *Debrief: Discuss the experience with your partner. Ask questions such as:*

- *How did it feel to be the guide or blindfolded participant?*

- *Was there clear communication throughout the activity?*

- *Did you trust your partner? If not, why?*

- *What did you learn about your partner during the activity?*

- *How can you apply what you learned in the activity to your relationship?*

7. *Reflect: Take time to reflect on the activity and the insights gained. Consider how you can apply the lessons learned to improve communication and trust in your relationship.*

The couple obstacle course activity is a fun and engaging way to improve communication and rebuild trust in your relationship. By working together and relying on each other, you can strengthen your bond and deepen your connection. Remember to practice clear communication and establish trust to navigate any obstacle course that comes your way.

Write Your Feelings

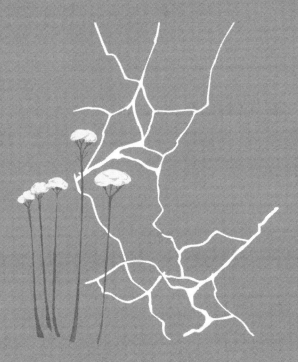

I am here with you,
because kind healing takes time.

Sending Signals

Worksheet

The Sending Signals method is a step-by-step approach to Recovering affair through interactive activities. Here are the steps:

Step 1: Acknowledge the Betrayal

The first step in regaining trust is to acknowledge the betrayal that occurred. Both parties need to have an open and honest discussion about what happened and how it impacted the relationship. This step is important because it helps to establish a shared understanding of the situation and allows both parties to express their feelings about the betrayal.

Step 2: Apologize

The person who broke the trust needs to take responsibility for their actions and apologize. A sincere apology involves admitting fault, expressing regret, and making a commitment to change. The person who was betrayed needs to be willing to accept the apology and acknowledge that the other person is taking responsibility for their actions.

Step 3: Identify the Signals of Trustworthiness

In this step, both parties need to identify the signals of trustworthiness that are important to them. This may include things like being honest and transparent, keeping promises, and being reliable. By identifying these signals, both parties can understand what they need to do to rebuild trust.

Step 4: Send Signals of Trustworthiness

Once the signals of trustworthiness have been identified, both parties need to work together to send these signals. This may involve actions like being more open and transparent, following through on commitments, and being consistent in behavior. The key is to consistently send signals of trustworthiness over time, as this will help to rebuild trust in the relationship.

It's important to regularly check in and monitor progress in rebuilding trust. This may involve having regular discussions about how both parties are feeling, and whether or not the signals of trustworthiness are being received. If one person feels like the other is not following through on their commitments, it's important to address this and work to find a solution together.

Step 6: Celebrate Successes

As progress is made in rebuilding trust, it's important to celebrate successes along the way. This may involve acknowledging when the other person has followed through on a commitment or shown a signal of trustworthiness. Celebrating successes helps to reinforce positive behavior and encourages both parties to continue working towards rebuilding trust.

The Sending Signals method is a step-by-step approach to Recovering affair through interactive activities. By acknowledging the betrayal, apologizing, identifying signals of trustworthiness, sending these signals, monitoring progress, and celebrating successes, both parties can work together to rebuild trust in their relationship.

Write Your Feelings

Antidotes for Hatred

The Antidotes for Hatred Method is an effective approach to Recovering affair through interactive activities. This method focuses on promoting positive emotions and building empathy between individuals who have experienced hurt or betrayal. It helps in addressing the negative emotions of hatred, anger, and resentment and promoting positive emotions of love, forgiveness, and empathy. This worksheet will help you.

Step 1: Acknowledge Your Emotions

The first step in the Antidotes for Hatred Method is to acknowledge your emotions. Take time to reflect on the emotions you are feeling towards the person who has hurt you. Write down your feelings, and be honest with yourself about how you feel.

Step 2: Identify the Cause of Your Emotions

The second step is to identify the cause of your emotions. Think about what the other person did that hurt you, and write it down. Be specific about the actions or words that caused your emotions.

Step 3: Practice Mindfulness

The third step is to practice mindfulness. Take time to sit quietly and focus on your breath. Notice any thoughts or emotions that arise, but do not judge them. Simply observe them and let them pass.

Step 4: Cultivate Positive Emotions

The fourth step is to cultivate positive emotions. Think about positive memories or experiences you have had with the person who hurt you. Focus on the positive emotions you felt during those times, such as love, joy, and gratitude. Write down these memories and emotions.

Step 5: Practice Empathy

The fifth step is to practice empathy. Try to understand their perspective. Think why they have acted and what they might have been feeling at the time. Write down your thoughts and feelings about their perspective.

Step 6: Practice Forgiveness

The sixth step is to practice forgiveness. This does not mean forgetting what the person did, but rather, it means letting go of the negative emotions associated with the hurt. Write down your feelings about forgiveness and what it means to you.

Step 7: Plan for Positive Actions

The final step is to plan for positive actions. Think about what positive actions you can take towards the other person to rebuild trust and improve the relationship. Write down your ideas and make a plan to put them into action.

Write Your Feelings

--.

Chapter 5

Difficulty in Dealing with Jealousy and Insecurity

Problem: Difficult to deal with jealousy? Try these exercises

Imago Relationship Treatment

Imago Relationship Treatment offers a worksheet to assist people with managing envy and frailty in their connections. This worksheet is intended to help people distinguish and communicate their sentiments, figure out the wellspring of their envy and weakness, and speak with their accomplice in a valuable and successful manner. Here utilizing the Image worksheet:

Stage 1: Recognize Your Sentiments

The initial step is to recognize and recognize your sensations of desire and uncertainty. Record how you feel and be all around as unambiguous as could be expected. For instance, "I feel envious when my accomplice converses with others at gatherings" or "I feel shaky when my accomplice invests energy with their ex."

Stage 2: Figure out the Wellspring of Your Sentiments

Investigate the wellspring of your desire and frailty. What sets off these sentiments? Is it a previous encounter, an absence of trust, or something different? Record your considerations and sentiments about the wellspring of your envy and instability.

Stage 3: Assume a sense of ownership with Your Sentiments

Assuming a sense of ownership with your sentiments and not fault your accomplice for them is significant. Record how you can get a sense of ownership with your

sentiments and convey them in a non-accusing manner. For instance, rather than saying "You cause me to feel desirous," have a go at saying "I feel envious when you invest energy with others."

Stage 4: Speak with Your Accomplice

Convey your sentiments and requirements to your accomplice in a useful and successful manner. Use "I" articulations to communicate how you feel and what you really want from your accomplice. Request their help and understanding. For instance, "I feel desirous when you converse with others at parties. Could we at any point make an arrangement together to assist me with feeling more great in those circumstances?"

Stage 5: Pay attention to Your Accomplice

Pay attention to your accomplice's reaction and attempt to grasp their point of view. Ask them how they feel and what they need from you. Show compassion and approve their sentiments. For instance, "I comprehend that you need to converse with others at parties. I simply need a consolation and backing to feel more great."

Stage 6: Practice Sympathy and Understanding

Practice sympathy and understanding towards your accomplice and yourself. Perceive that envy and uncertainty are normal feelings that everybody encounters on occasion. Show restraint toward yourself and your accomplice as you work through these sentiments together.

Write Your Feelings

Partner 1	Partner 2

Valuing Your Partner

Desire is an ordinary inclination, yet it very well may be overpowering and challenging to make due. It can prompt sensations of weakness, question, and harm the relationship. Assuming that you battle with envy, this worksheet will assist you with perceiving the triggers, figure out the basic feelings, and learn methodologies to oversee desire and worth your accomplice.

Stage 1: *Distinguishing Triggers Recognize the circumstances or ways of behaving that trigger desire. Record the triggers that cause you to feel desirous, for example, your accomplice investing energy with companions, conversing with somebody alluring, or not answering your messages immediately.*

Stage 2: *Understanding the Hidden Feelings Desire is in many cases driven by basic feelings, like weakness, separation anxiety, or low confidence. Record the feelings that you experience when you feel desirous. For instance, do you feel restless, irate, miserable, or deficient?*

Stage 3: *Testing Negative Considerations Desire is in many cases energized by bad contemplations, for example, "my accomplice doesn't cherish me," "I'm not adequate," or "my accomplice will leave me for somebody better." Challenge these negative considerations by inquiring as to whether they depend on proof or suppositions. Are there any elective clarifications for your accomplice's way of behaving? What might a believed companion say regarding your contemplations?*

Stage 4: *Rehearsing Taking care of oneself Desire can be genuinely depleting and can influence your prosperity. Practice taking care of oneself by participating in exercises that encourage you, like working out, thinking, investing energy with companions, or seeking after a leisure activity.*

Stage 5: *Speaking with Your Accomplice Open correspondence with your accomplice is fundamental to overseeing desire. Converse with your accomplice about your sentiments, triggers, and techniques for overseeing envy. Be explicit about what ways of behaving or circumstances trigger envy and what support you want from your accomplice.*

Stage 6: *Esteeming Your Accomplice Desire can make a negative pattern of question and uncertainty in the relationship. Center around esteeming your accomplice by recognizing their positive characteristics and offering thanks for their activities. Record three things that you value about your accomplice, like their comical inclination, their benevolence, or their help.*

Stage 7: *Observing Your Relationship Desire can make you center around the negatives in the relationship, however commending the positives is significant. Record three things that you love about your relationship, like shared interests, correspondence, or closeness.*

Stage 8: *Rehearsing Appreciation can assist with moving your concentration from negative to positive parts of the relationship. Record that you are thankful for in your relationship, like your accomplice's affection, backing, or responsibility.*

Stage 9: *Putting forth Objectives Laying out objectives can assist you with zeroing in on sure ways of behaving and results. Record three objectives for overseeing desire and esteeming your accomplice, for example, rehearsing taking care of oneself consistently, testing negative considerations, or offering thanks day to day.*

Stage 10: *Investigating Progress Audit your advancement routinely and commend your accomplishments. Evaluate the adequacy of your techniques and change them depending on the situation. Look for help from a confided in companion or a specialist if important.*

Write Your Feelings

The Big Picture

The Big Picture Partners Worksheet is a tool that helps partners in a relationship to gain a deeper understanding of each other's values, goals, and priorities. By completing this worksheet together, partners can identify areas where they may have different perspectives and work towards creating a shared vision for their future together.

Here's a guide on how to complete the Big Picture Partners Worksheet:

1. *Start by setting aside some dedicated time for you and your partner to work through this worksheet together. Find a corner where you won't be distracted .*

2. *Begin by reflecting on your own values, goals, and priorities. What is most important to you in life? What are your long-term goals for yourself and your relationship? Write down your thoughts and ideas on the worksheet.*

3. *Once you've completed your own section of the worksheet, share your answers with your partner. Encourage them to listen attentively and ask questions to clarify any points they may not understand.*

4. *Next, it's your partner's turn to share their values, goals, and priorities. Listen carefully and ask questions to gain a deeper understanding of their perspective.*

5. *As you both share your thoughts and ideas, look for areas where you may have different perspectives. These differences are perfectly normal and can be the source of great growth in your relationship. Use this opportunity to explore these differences and find ways to work together towards common goals.*

6. *Once you've shared your individual perspectives, work together to create a vision for your future. This can include shared values, goals, and priorities that you both agree are important for your relationship.*

7. *Finally, commit to revisiting this worksheet periodically to check in on your progress towards your shared vision. This can help you stay aligned and continue to work towards your goals as a team.*

Completing the Big Picture Partners Worksheet can be a powerful tool for building trust and understanding in your relationship. By gaining a deeper understanding of each other's values, goals, and priorities, you can work together towards a shared vision for your future together.

Write Your Feelings

The Ranking Exercise in Couples

Introduction: In order to enhance communication and strengthen the relationship between partners, it's important to be able to understand each other's priorities and preferences. This is where the Ranking Exercise comes in handy. This exercise involves ranking a list of items or activities in order of importance to each partner, and then discussing the rankings together.

Instructions:

1. *Begin by making a list of items or activities that are important to your relationship. This can include things like communication, intimacy, quality time, household chores, personal hobbies, and career goals.*

2. *Each partner should then rank these items or activities in order of importance to them, starting with the most important and ending with the least important.*

3. *Once both partners have completed their rankings, compare them side by side. Take note of any similarities or differences in the rankings.*

4. *Discuss the reasons behind your rankings. Why did you rank certain items higher or lower than your partner? What do these rankings say about your priorities and preferences in the relationship?*

5. *Work together to create a shared ranking that takes into account both partners' perspectives. This may involve compromise and negotiation, but the goal is to find a ranking that both partners are satisfied with.*

6. *Finally, use the rankings as a guide for future decisions and actions in your relationship. Keep in mind each other's priorities and preferences when making plans or addressing issues that may arise.*

Tips:

- *Be honest and open when completing the rankings. Don't feel pressured to rank items a certain way just because you think it's what your partner wants to hear.*

- *Listen actively to your partner's explanations for their rankings. Try to get their perspective even if it's different from your own.*

- *Remember that this exercise is meant to enhance communication and understanding in your relationship, not to cause conflict. Keep the conversation respectful and constructive.*

The Ranking Exercise is a useful tool for couples to gain a better understanding of each other's priorities and preferences. By completing this exercise together, partners can create a shared ranking that reflects their mutual goals and values in the relationship. This can help to strengthen communication and trust between partners, and improve overall relationship satisfaction.

Write Your Feelings

Partner 1	Partner 2

The Pause That Refreshes

Introduction: The pause that refreshes in couples is a crucial tool to develop a deeper level of communication and understanding in a relationship. This worksheet is designed to help couples practice the pause that refreshes technique in their everyday lives, to promote better communication and strengthen their bond.

Instructions:

1. *Find a calm place so you can have a conversation with your partner without any distractions.*

2. *Begin by acknowledging your partner's perspective and feelings, and make sure they feel heard.*

3. Take a deep breath and consciously let go of any tension or negative emotions you may be feeling.

4. Practice active listening by paraphrasing what your partner has said and reflecting on how it makes you feel.

5. Ask questions to get understanding of your partner's thoughts and emotions.

6. Take deep breath and permit yourself to fully process and respond to what your partner has shared.

7. Share your perspective in a calm and respectful manner, focusing on your feelings and thoughts rather than blaming or attacking your partner.

8. Take turns practicing the pause that refreshes technique, allowing each other to speak and be heard without interruption.

Discussion:

1. How did it feel to practice the pause that refreshes technique? Did it improve your communication and understanding of your partner's perspective?

2. What are some situations where using the pause that refreshes technique could be especially helpful in your relationship?

3. How can you incorporate the pause that refreshes technique into your daily communication with your partner?

4. What are some potential challenges you may face when practicing the pause that refreshes technique, and how can you overcome them?

Conclusion: The pause that refreshes in couples is a powerful tool for promoting deeper communication and understanding in a relationship. By practicing this technique regularly, you and your partner can strengthen your bond and build a stronger foundation for a fulfilling and long-lasting relationship. Remember to approach each conversation with willingness to listen and understand your partner's perspective.

Write Your Feelings

--.

Getting the Envy Root

Desire is a typical inclination experienced by people in a heartfelt connection. It can emerge from a feeling of dread toward losing one's accomplice, feeling unreliable, or seeing a danger to the relationship. Despite the fact that envy might appear as though a characteristic reaction, it tends to be disastrous and harmful to the relationship. Accordingly, it is fundamental to distinguish the main driver of desire and address it to forestall any further harm to the relationship. The accompanying worksheet is intended to assist couples with getting to the foundation of their desire issues and track down ways of tending to them.

Stage 1: Recognize the Triggers

Record the circumstances or ways of behaving that trigger your sensations of envy. Be explicit and definite in your depictions. For instance, on the off chance that your accomplice invests energy with their ex, record how you feel and what contemplations ring a bell.

Stage 2: Distinguish the Basic Convictions

Investigate the convictions that underlie your desire. These convictions might be founded on previous encounters, weaknesses, or presumptions. Record what you understand regarding yourself, your accomplice, and the relationship when you experience envy. For example, you might accept that you are not adequate for your accomplice or that your accomplice isn't dependable.

Stage 3: Challenge Your Convictions

Look at your convictions and question their legitimacy. Inquire as to whether they are exact or they depend on unwarranted suppositions. Challenge your convictions by giving proof that goes against them. For instance, in the event that you accept that your accomplice isn't reliable, help yourself to remember the times when they have told the truth and devoted.

Stage 4: Speak with Your Accomplice

Discuss your thoughts and contemplations with your accomplice in a quiet and conscious way. Make sense of what sets off your desire and what hidden convictions add to it. Be available to their viewpoint and pay attention to their criticism. Attempt to figure out some shared interest and work together to track down arrangements.

Stage 5: Form Trust

Trust is fundamental in any relationship. In the event that trust is deficient with regards to, desire can turn into a critical issue. In this manner, it is urgent to chip away at building entrust with your accomplice. Examine ways of building trust, for example, tell the truth, keeping guarantees, and being dependable.

Stage 6: Practice Taking care of oneself

Desire can be unpleasant and sincerely depleting. Thusly, dealing with yourself is essential. Participate in exercises that cause you to feel far better and lessen pressure, like activity, reflection, or investing energy with companions.

All in all, desire is a complicated feeling that can harm a relationship in the event that not tended to. By recognizing the triggers, hidden convictions, and correspondence with your accomplice, you can focus on the heart of the matter and track down ways of tending to it. Building trust and rehearsing taking care of oneself can likewise assist with beating envy and reinforce the relationship.

Write Your Feelings

Reaching a Positive Outcome in Relationships despite Adversity

Relationships can be difficult and it's not uncommon for adversity to arise. These difficulties can come in many forms, from external factors such as financial struggles or job loss, to internal factors like communication issues or disagreements over values. Whatever the cause, adversity can put a strain on a relationship and make it difficult to maintain a positive outlook. However, there are things challenges and reach a positive outcome in your relationship.

One of the most important steps in reaching a positive outcome is communication. It's crucial to be open and honest with your partner about your thoughts and feelings. This means to listen their perspective and finding a way to work together towards a solution. For It's also important to express appreciation and gratitude towards your partner, even in difficult times. This can help to bring a sense of closeness and increase the chances of finding a positive outcome.

Another important aspect is maintaining a positive attitude. This doesn't mean ignoring the challenges or pretending that everything is fine when it isn't. Instead, it means choosing to focus on what can be done to improve the situation, rather than dwelling on the negative. This can involve finding small things to be grateful for, such as a supportive friend or a moment of laughter with your partner. By focusing on the positive, you can build resilience and increase your ability to navigate difficult situations. It's also important to be willing to seek outside help if needed. This could mean therapist or counselor to help navigate the challenges in your relationship. It could also mean reaching out to friends or family members for support. Whatever the source of help, it's important to be willing to accept it and to work together to find solutions. Finally, it's important to recognize that reaching a positive outcome takes time and effort. It's not anything that will occur overnight, and there may be setbacks along the way. However, by staying committed to open communication, maintaining a positive attitude, and seeking outside help when needed, it's possible to navigate adversity and reach a positive outcome in your relationship. Reaching a positive outcome in relationships despite adversity requires open communication, a positive attitude, willingness to seek outside help, and recognition that it takes time and effort. By working together with your partner and staying committed to these principles, you can navigate even the most difficult challenges and come out stronger on the other side.

Chapter 6

Maintaining a healthy relationship

Keeping a sound relationship is essential for a dependable and satisfying organization. It includes investing steady energy, correspondence, shared regard, and an eagerness to deal with difficulties together. Here are a few critical tips and systems for keeping a sound relationship:

Correspondence: Transparent correspondence is fundamental in any relationship. It's critical to have the option to offer your viewpoints, sentiments, and necessities unafraid of judgment or kickback. It's likewise pivotal to be a decent audience and focus on what your accomplice is talking about. Make time to talk routinely and examine any issues or worries that might emerge.

Regard: Shared regard is the groundwork of a solid relationship. Regard each other's sentiments, conclusions, and limits. Keep away from verbally abusing, affronts, or other discourteous way of behaving, and center around treating your band together with thoughtfulness and sympathy.

Quality time: Getting to know each other is fundamental for keeping a solid relationship. Try to do exercises that you both partake in and make new encounters together. This could be anything from going for a climb, preparing supper together, or basically going through a calm night at home.

Trust: Trust is a basic part of a sound relationship. It's fundamental to be straightforward with one another and completely finish responsibilities. Assuming trust has been broken, it's critical to figure out through the problem and remake it.

Split the difference: Connections require split the difference from the two players. Finding a harmony between your singular requirements and the necessities of the relationship is significant. Think twice about little issues and work together to track down answers for bigger ones.

Taking care of oneself: Dealing with yourself is fundamental for keeping a sound relationship. Set aside a few minutes for exercises that give you pleasure and focus on your physical and emotional wellness. At the point when you deal with yourself, you are better ready to appear for your accomplice and the relationship.

Absolution: Pardoning is a significant piece of any relationship. It's vital to have the option to pardon your accomplice for mix-ups and push ahead together. Be that as it may, absolution doesn't mean neglecting or permitting a similar way of behaving to proceed.

Generally, keeping a solid relationship requires progressing exertion, correspondence, and common regard. By focusing on these you can make serious areas of strength for a satisfying organization that endures.

Problem: For having hard time in maintaining the relationship? Try these

Spend 15 minutes hugging

Cuddling is a simple yet powerful way for couples to show affection, reduce stress, and improve their overall well-being. This worksheet is designed to help couples incorporate regular cuddling into their relationship.

Step 1: Set a Goal Discuss with your partner how often you would like to cuddle each week. Set a goal that is realistic and achievable for both of you. For example, you might aim to cuddle for 15 minutes each day before bed, or for 30 minutes twice a week.

Step 2: Create a Cuddle Space Choose a comfortable and cozy spot in your home where you can cuddle without distractions. Make sure the space is clean, quiet, and free from any electronics or other distractions. You might choose to lay down on a soft blanket or couch, or sit in a comfortable chair.

Step 3: Get Comfortable Before you start cuddling, make sure you and your partner are both comfortable. Remove any uncomfortable clothing or items that may be in the way. You might want to wear comfortable clothes or pajamas. Get into a comfortable position, such as spooning or facing each other, whichever works best for you.

Step 4: Set the Mood Create a relaxing and romantic atmosphere by dimming the lights or lighting candles. Play some nature sounds to help you and your partner relax and get in the mood for cuddling.

Step 5: Start Cuddling Begin by holding hands or hugging each other. Take deep breaths and focus on the present moment. Start by cuddling for 5-10 minutes and gradually increase the time as you both become more comfortable. Use this time to talk, share your feelings, or simply enjoy each other's company.

Step 6: End on a Positive Note When your cuddle time is over, take a few moments to express your gratitude to your partner for spending time with you. Share any positive thoughts or feelings you had during the cuddle session. You might even want to set a date for your next cuddle session.

Step 7: Practice Regularly Make cuddling a regular part of your routine. Stick to the goal you set in Step 1, and try to make cuddling a priority in your relationship. Keep in mind that cuddling can also be a great way to bond and reconnect after an argument or disagreement.

Remember that cuddling is a simple yet powerful way to improve your relationship and your overall well-being. Use this worksheet as a guide to make cuddling a regular and enjoyable part of your relationship.

Write Your Feelings

Regular dating nights

Objective: The purpose of this worksheet is to help couples establish regular date nights to strengthen their relationship and maintain a healthy and happy partnership.

Instructions:

Step 1: Discuss and decide on a specific day and time for regular date nights. Make sure that both partners are available and committed to this plan.

Step 2: Choose a location or activity for your date night. This can be as simple as cooking dinner together at home or trying a new restaurant in town. It's important to mix up your activities to keep things interesting.

Step 3: Plan your date night activities in advance. Decide on a theme for each date night or choose activities that you both enjoy. For example, you can have a movie night, game night, or try a new outdoor activity.

Step 4: Hold each other accountable. Encourage each other and make date night a priority. Avoid canceling or rescheduling unless it's absolutely necessary.

Step 5: Use date night to connect with each other. Put away your phones and focus on spending quality time together. Share your thoughts, feelings, and experiences with each other.

Step 6: Reflect on your date nights. After each date night, take some time to reflect on what you enjoyed and what you can improve on. Use this feedback to plan future date nights.

Step 7: Be open to trying new things. Don't be afraid to come out of your zone and try new activities. This can help you learn more about each other and strengthen your bond.

Step 8: Keep the romance alive. Make an effort to show your love and affection for each other. This can be as simple as holding hands or giving each other compliments.

Conclusion: Regular date nights can help couples maintain a healthy and happy relationship. By committing to this plan and holding each other accountable, you can strengthen your bond and create lasting memories together.

Bonus Tip: If you have children, consider scheduling a regular babysitter or asking a family member to watch them during your date nights. This will give you and your partner some much-needed alone time to reconnect and enjoy each other's company.

Write Your Feelings

Partner 1	Partner 2

Together, try something novel

"Together, trying something novel" is a worksheet designed to encourage couples to explore new experiences and activities together. By engaging in novel activities, couples can strengthen their bond, improve communication, and create new shared memories. Here is a guide to complete this worksheet:

Step 1: *Brainstorm a list of activities*

The main step is to write with a list of activities that you and your partner have never done before. This could include things like trying a new cuisine, taking a dance class, going on a hot air balloon ride, or exploring a new city. Make a list of at least five activities that you both find interesting and exciting.

Step 2: *Choose an activity Next, choose one activity from the list that you both agree to try. It should be something that you both feel comfortable with and excited* *about. Make sure to schedule a date and time for the activity so that you have a concrete plan in place.*

Step 3: *Discuss your expectations Before embarking on the activity, take some time to discuss your expectations. What do you hope to gain from the experience? What do you want to get individually and as a couple? Make affirm you are both on the same page and have a clear understanding of what you want to achieve.*

Step 4: *Reflect on the experience After completing the activity, take some time to reflect on the experience. How did you feel during the activity? Did it meet your expectations? What did you learn about your partner? Discuss your thoughts and feelings with each other, and be open and honest about your experience.*

Step 5: *Plan the next activity Now that you have completed one novel activity, it's time to plan the next one. Use the same process as before to brainstorm and choose an activity that you both want to try. Repeat until you have finished all the activities on your list.*

Step 6: *Keep the momentum going Once you have completed all the activities on your list, it's important to keep the momentum going. Make it a habit to regularly try new things together, whether it's exploring a new city or trying a new restaurant. By continuously engaging in novel experiences, you can keep your relationship fresh and exciting.*

In conclusion, the "Together, trying something novel" worksheet is a great way for couples to strengthen their bond and create new shared memories. By coming out of your zone and trying new things together, you can maintain a healthy and exciting relationship.

Write Your Feelings

Finishing a cooperative project

Congratulations on embarking on a cooperative project with your partner! Working together towards a shared goal can be a great way to strengthen your relationship and create something meaningful together. However, finishing a project can sometimes be challenging, especially when two people are involved. This worksheet will assist you through the process of finishing your cooperative project successfully.

Step 1: *Clarify Your Goals Before you can finish your project, it's essential to clarify what you're trying to accomplish. Ask yourself and your partner the following questions:*

1. *What was the original goal of this project?*

2. *Has this goal changed since we started working on the project?*

3. *What do we hope to achieve by finishing this project?*

Once you've answered these questions, write down your goals and make sure that you and your partner are on the same page.

Step 2: *Define Your Roles To finish your project successfully, you need to be clear about who is responsible for what. Sit down with your partner and discuss the following questions:*

1. *What are each of our strengths and weaknesses?*

2. How can we use our strengths to contribute to the project?

3. What tasks are each of us responsible for?

4. How will we communicate with each other throughout the project?

Write down your roles and responsibilities and make sure that you both understand and agree with them.

Step 3: *Create a Timeline One of the most effective ways to finish a project is to set a timeline for completion. Sit down with and create a timeline that includes the following:*

1. A beginning date and last date for the project

2. Milestones or checkpoints along the way

3. Tasks that need to be completed each week or month

4. Deadlines for each task

Make sure that your timeline is realistic and that it takes into account any other commitments that you or your partner have.

Step 4: *Stay Motivated Finishing a project can be challenging, and it's essential to stay motivated throughout the process. Here are some tips to assist your partner in staying motivated:*

1. Celebrate your successes along the way

2. Set small goals and reward yourselves when you achieve them

3. Take breaks and make sure to rest and recharge

4. Remind yourselves of the benefits of finishing the project

Step 5: *Communicate Communication is key to finishing a project successfully. Here are some tricks for communicating efficiently with your partner:*

1. Schedule check-ins on any challenges you're facing

2. Be open and honest about your feelings and opinions

3. Listen actively and be willing to compromise

4. Celebrate each other's contributions and successes

Step 6: *Finish Strong As you approach the end of your project, it's important to stay focused and finish strong. Here are some tricks to help you do that:*

1. Review your timeline and make sure that you're on track to finish on time

2. Double-check that all tasks are complete and that nothing has been overlooked

3. Make any final adjustments or revisions as needed

4. Celebrate your accomplishment and take time to reflect on what you've achieved together

Conclusion: *Finishing a cooperative project with your partner can be an incredibly rewarding experience. By clarifying your goals, defining your roles, creating a timeline, staying motivated, communicating effectively, and finishing strong, you can achieve your shared goal and strengthen your relationship in the process. Use this worksheet to assist you and your partner in finishing your project successfully.*

Write Your Feelings

Partner 1	Partner 2

Scavenger hunts can be a tomfoolery and an invigorating way for couples to know each other while investigating new spots and finding stowed-away fortunes. Here is a worksheet to assist you with arranging your own scavenger chase experience:

Pick your area

Choose where you need to have your scavenger chase. It very well may be in a recreation area, a gallery, a midtown region, or even in your own home. Ensure it's a spot that both you and your accomplice will appreciate investigating.

Make your pieces of information.

Think of a progression of pieces of information that will lead your accomplice to every area. Make them trying, however not excessively troublesome. Use conundrums, riddles, and wit to keep things fascinating. You can likewise add a heartfelt touch to the signs by integrating inside jokes or recollections you have shared.

Settle on the award

Figure out what the award will be for finishing the scavenger chase. It very well may be a heartfelt supper, an end-of-the-week escape, or something less difficult like a hand-crafted dessert. Pick something that will spur your accomplice to complete the scavenger chase.

Put down a point in time limit

Conclude how long you need the scavenger chase to endure. It very well may be 60 minutes, a portion of a day, or even an entire day. Ensure you give your accomplice sufficient opportunity to finish the chase without feeling surged.

Go on the chase!

Upon the arrival of the scavenger chase, provide your accomplice the primary insight and watch as they set off on their experience. Follow them at a protected distance to perceive how they are advancing and to ensure they don't get lost. Whenever they have finished the last sign, shock them with the award!

Interview

After the scavenger chase is finished, carve out opportunity to interview with your accomplice. Get some information about their #1 hints and areas, and what they saw as generally testing. Utilize this input to further develop future scavenger hunts.

A few extra tips to make your scavenger chase a triumph:

Be imaginative with your signs. Utilize a wide range of kinds of signs to keep things fascinating.

Ensure your accomplice has all that they need to finish the scavenger chase, like a guide, a pen, and a telephone with a camera.

Try not to make the scavenger chase excessively troublesome. You believe that your accomplice should partake in the experience, not feel disappointed.

Be ready for any weather patterns. Bring an umbrella, sunscreen, or some other important things relying on the area.

Have some good times! Scavenger hunts are intended to be a tomfoolery and invigorating experience for both you and your accomplice. Partake in the experience!

Write Your Feelings

Having a trust discussion

Introduction:

Trust is main component in any relationship, particularly in heartfelt connections. At the point when accomplices trust one another, it makes serious areas of strength for a for the relationship to flourish. In any case, now and again trust can be broken, prompting sensations of harmed, selling out, and frailty. Hence, it is fundamental for couples to have transparent discussions about trust to keep a solid relationship. This worksheet will direct you through the most common way of having a trust conversation with your accomplice.

Stage 1: Recognize the Significance of Trust

Pause for a minute to ponder what trust means for your relationship. Pose yourself the accompanying inquiries:

What's the significance here to you?

How has trust assumed a part in your relationship up until this point?

What are a few advantages of having trust in a relationship?

What are a few outcomes of lacking trust in a relationship?

Share your responses with your accomplice and pay attention to their reactions. Examine how you both worth trust and why it means a lot to your relationship.

Stage 2: Distinguish Areas of Trust

Trust is definitely not a solitary idea yet a mix of various elements. To have a useful trust conversation, it is fundamental to recognize explicit areas of trust that might be pertinent to your relationship. An areas of trust that you might need to consider include:

Profound trust: the capacity to trust in one another and feel sincerely upheld

Sexual trust: the capacity to be transparent about sexual longings and inclinations

Monetary trust: the capacity to trust each other with cash and monetary choices

Social trust: the capacity to trust each other's way of behaving and activities in friendly circumstances

Individual trust: the capacity to trust each other's personality and respectability

Distinguish which areas of trust are generally critical to your relationship and examine how you can further develop them if necessary.

Stage 3: Offer Worries and Encounters

Sharing your interests and encounters connected with trust can assist with building a more profound comprehension and sympathy among you and your accomplice. Think about the accompanying inquiries:

Have you at any point encountered a break of trust in a past relationship?

Have you at any point felt like your accomplice has penetrated your trust in this relationship?

Are there any activities or ways of behaving that cause you to have an uncomfortable or unreliable outlook on trust?

Sharing your interests in a non-critical and deferential way is significant. Use "I" articulations and try not to fault or blaming your accomplice. Permit your accomplice to share their own encounters and concerns, and listen effectively to what they need to say.

Stage 4: Examine Limits and Assumptions

Limits and assumptions are basic in any relationship, and they assume a significant part in laying out trust. Talk about with your accomplice what you both anticipate from one another and what limits you really want to have a good sense of reassurance and secure in the relationship. Think about the accompanying inquiries:

What ways of behaving or activities are OK or unsatisfactory in the relationship?

How long and space do you have to feel great and secure in the relationship?

Are there a particular assumptions you have about correspondence or straightforwardness?

Speak the truth about what you really want and pay attention to your accomplice's requirements also. Laying out clear limits and assumptions can assist with forestalling false impressions and miscommunications.

Stage 5: Resolve to Trust-Building Activities

Having a trust conversation is an extraordinary initial step, however vital to circle back to activities exhibit your obligation to building and keeping up with trust in your relationship. Think about the accompanying activities:

Be transparent with one another, in any event, when it's troublesome.

Stay faithful to your obligations and completely finish responsibilities.

Show compassion and understanding when your accomplice shares their interests.

Stay away from activities or ways of behaving that might harm trust.

Persistently speak with one another and monitor how you're both inclination about the relationship.

End:

Having a trust conversation can be testing, however it is entertaining.

Write Your Feelings

Crazy Game Night

Introduction

Game nights are a fun way for couples to spend quality time together and bond over shared interests. In this worksheet, we will explore different ideas for a Crazy Game Night that will challenge and entertain couples.

Game Ideas:

Minute to Win It - In this game, couples will compete against each other in a series of one-minute challenges using household items. For example, see who can stack the most cups in one minute, or who can balance the most cookies on their forehead.

Truth or Dare - This classic game can be a lot of fun for couples. Take turns regarding truth questions or daring each other to do silly or embarrassing things. Just be sure to keep it lighthearted and fun!

Pictionary - This drawing game is perfect for couples who are competitive and love to show off their artistic skills. Use a whiteboard or paper and markers to draw clues for your partner to guess.

Charades - In this classic game, one partner acts out a word without speaking, while the other partner tries to guess what they are acting out. This game can be a lot of fun and is perfect for couples who love to be silly and creative.

Board Games - There are great board games out there that are perfect for couples. Whether you love strategy games like Risk or Settlers of Catan, or classic games like Scrabble or Monopoly, there is sure to be a game that you will both enjoy.

A Crazy Game Night for couples is best to spend quality time together and bond over shared interests. Whether you choose to play Minute to Win It, Truth or Dare, Pictionary, Charades, or board games, you are sure to have a lot of fun and make some great memories. So why not plan your next game night today and get ready for some crazy fun!

Trying Nature Hike

Objective:

The objective of this worksheet is to direct couples on the best way to design and partake in a nature climb together. Through this action, couples will have a valuable chance to investigate the outside, interface with nature, and develop their bond with one another.

Materials:

Happy with strolling shoes

Fitting apparel for the climate (for example downpour coat, sun cap, and so forth.)

Sunscreen and bug splash

Water container and bites

Guide or GPS gadget

Discretionary: optics, camera, climbing posts

Guidelines:

Pick a path: *Exploration neighborhood trails that are reasonable for your wellness level and interests. Consider factors, for example, distance, rise gain, landscape, and view. Pick a path that you both feel OK with and eager to investigate.*

Plan your course: *Utilize a guide or GPS gadget to design your course before you set out on your climb. Try to take note of any significant milestones, mood killers, or likely perils en route. Plan to begin your climb promptly in the first part of the day to keep away from swarms and the late morning heat.*

Pack your stuff: *Make an agenda of fundamental things you'll require for your climb, and pack them in a knapsack. Carry a lot of water and snacks to keep your energy steps up. Wear open to strolling shoes and dress in layers to plan for changes in climate. Remember to apply sunscreen and bug splash depending on the situation.*

Play it safe: *Before you set out on your climb, ensure somebody knows your course and assessed bring time back. Bring an emergency treatment unit in the event of injury, and be ready to change your arrangements assuming circumstances change out of the blue.*

Partake in the climb: *When you start your climb, find opportunity to see the value in the regular magnificence around you. Connect with your faculties by noticing the vegetation, paying attention to the hints of the backwoods, and feeling the breeze on your skin. Enjoy reprieves on a case by case basis to rest, hydrate, and refuel.*

Interface with your accomplice: *Utilize the time on your climb to associate with your accomplice. Participate in discussion, clasp hands, or essentially appreciate each other's conversation peacefully. Take photographs or recordings to archive your experience and make recollections together.*

Practice Leave No Follow: *As you climb, be aware of your effect on the climate. Follow Leave No Follow standards by pressing out all rubbish, remaining on assigned trails, and regarding untamed life and vegetation.*

Think about your experience: After your climb, carve out opportunity to consider your experience together. Examine what you delighted in about the climb, what challenges you confronted, and what you realized. Utilize this valuable chance to extend your association with one another and with nature.

End:

A nature climb is a superb way for couples to get to know each other while partaking in the magnificence of the outside. By preparing, playing it safe, and rehearsing Leave No Follow, you can have a protected and charming experience. Find opportunity to interface with your accomplice and with nature, and utilize this chance to extend your bond with one another.

Write Your Experience

Partner 1	Partner 2

Perfect Art Class

Welcome to the Ideal Art Class for Couples Worksheet! This worksheet will assist with directing you through the means of arranging and partaking in an art class with your better half.

Stage 1: Pick the sort of art class

The initial step is to pick the sort of art class you might want to take together. Would you like to paint, draw, shape, or have a go at something different? Consider your inclinations, skill level, and how much time you have. Some well known art classes for couples include:

Paint and taste: a tomfoolery and loosened up painting class where you can partake in a glass of wine while you paint

Earthenware making: an involved class where you can make stoneware together

Drawing: a classic art class that permits you to communicate your imagination

Photography: a class where you can figure out how to take wonderful photographs together

Stage 2: Track down a class close to you

Whenever you have settled on the kind of art class you need to take, now is the ideal time to track down a class close to you. You can look online for art studios, public venues, or art schools in your space that offer the sort of class you need to take. A few classes might be offered for all intents and purposes, so you can likewise think about web-based choices.

Stage 3: Register for the class

Whenever you have found a class that you are keen on, now is the right time to enroll. Make a point to peruse the class portrayal cautiously and really take a look at the date, time, and area. Assuming that you have any inquiries, make sure to the teacher or the studio.

Stage 4: Plan for the class

Before the class, try to plan all that you will require. This might incorporate art supplies, open to apparel, and any bites or beverages you need to bring. Try to likewise clear your timetable so you can completely partake in the class with next to no interruptions.

Stage 5: Go to the class

Upon the arrival of the class, show up sooner than expected to give yourself a lot of opportunity to get settled. Make a point to acquaint yourself with the teacher and some other participants. During the class, have a great time and don't hesitate for even a moment to commit errors. Keep in mind, the mark of the class is to live it up and make something together.

Stage 6: Consider the experience

After the class, carve out opportunity to consider the experience. What did you appreciate about the class? What did you realize? Did you have a great time? Thinking about the experience can assist you with valuing the time you spent together and may try and rouse you to take one more class from now on.

Taking an art class with your life partner can be a tomfoolery and compensating experience. By following these means, you can design the ideal art class and partake in making something wonderful together.

Write Your Experience

A Karaoke Night

Karaoke nights can be a great way for couples to have fun, let loose, and sing their hearts out. Here is a worksheet that can help you plan a memorable karaoke night for you and your significant other.

Choose the venue: First, you need to choose the right venue for your karaoke night. Look for a local bar or restaurant that has a karaoke machine or a private karaoke room that you can rent. Make sure the venue has a good sound system and a wide selection of songs to choose from.

Pick the date and time: Decide on a date and time that works for both you and your partner. Make sure you choose a night when you both have time off from work and can relax and enjoy the evening.

Invite other couples: Consider inviting a few other couples to join you for the karaoke night. It can be fun to sing duets or group songs with friends, and it can also make the evening more festive.

Choose your songs: Take some time to choose your favorite songs to sing together. Look for songs that are romantic or have special meaning to your relationship. You can also choose some fun, upbeat songs to sing individually or with friends.

Practice your singing: If you're not comfortable singing in public, consider practicing your singing beforehand. You can sing along with the songs at home or even take singing lessons together to improve your skills.

Dress up: Make the evening special by dressing up for the occasion. Wear something comfortable, and consider matching your outfit with your partner's for a fun couple's look.

Bring snacks and drinks: Most venues will have drinks and snacks and you also bring your own. Consider bringing a bottle wine snacks to share with your partner and friends.

Have fun!: Finally, remember to have fun! Karaoke nights are all about letting loose and having a good time. Don't worry about being perfect or hitting all the *right notes. Just enjoy the experience and make some fun memories with your partner.*

By following these you can decide a fun and memorable karaoke night for you and your significant other. So grab the mic, sing your heart out, and have a great time!

Write Your Experience

A Spa Day

Here's a worksheet on planning a Spa Day for couples:

1. **Schedule:**

- *Decide on a date and time that works best for both of you.*

- *Consider the spa's availability and make a reservation ahead of time to ensure you get the treatments you want at the time you prefer.*

- *Plan for a few hours, or even a whole day, to truly relax and rejuvenate.*

2. **Choose your treatments:**

- *Look through the spa's menu of services and decide what treatments you want to book.*

- *Consider a couples massage, facials, body treatments, or anything else that catches your interest.*

- *Think about what you both enjoy and choose are treatments that will make you feel pampered and relaxed.*

3. **Pack your bags:**

- *Make a checklist of things to bring, including swimwear if there's a pool or hot tub, flip flops, a change of clothes, and any personal care items you may need.*

- *Pack light so you don't have to carry too much around.*

- *Don't forget to bring a book, magazine while you wait for your treatments.*

4. **Arrive early:**

- *Plan to arrive at the spa at least 30 minutes before your treatments to permit time for check-in, changing, and getting settled.*

- *Take advantage of any amenities offered, such as steam room, to assist you relax and unwind before your treatments.*

5. *Enjoy your treatments:*

- *Once your treatments begin, let go of any worries or distractions and focus on enjoying the experience.*

- *Communicate with your therapist about the pressure or technique to ensure the treatment is tailored to your preferences.*

- *Breathe deeply and allow yourself to fully relax and enjoy the moment.*

6. *Take advantage of other amenities:*

- *After your treatments, take some time to explore the spa's other amenities, such as a lounge area or outdoor pool.*

- *Sip on a refreshing drink or snack on some healthy bites to replenish your energy levels.*

- *Take time to reflect on how you feel and appreciate the time you've spent together.*

7. *Plan for some post-spa relaxation:*

- *After your spa day, plan for some post-spa relaxation time, whether it's a quiet dinner at home, a stroll in nature, or simply curling up on the couch together.*

- *Take time to reflect on the experience and the benefits you've gained from taking a break from your daily routine.*

Remember, a spa day for couples is not just about the treatments, it's about taking time to connect with each other and relax in a tranquil and serene environment. Enjoy the experience and cherish the memories you create together!

Write Your Experience

Creating a vision board

Making a vision board as a couple can be a fun and powerful activity that allows you to share your goals, aspirations, and dreams with each other. Here's a step-by-step guide to help you create a vision board together:

__Step 1:__ Set a Date and Time Pick a date and time that works for both of you. It's important to set aside enough time to complete the vision board without feeling rushed.

__Step 2:__ Gather Supplies Gather all the supplies you need for creating the vision board. You will need a poster board or canvas, magazines, scissors, glue or tape, markers or pens, and any other materials you want to use to decorate your board, such as stickers or glitter.

__Step 3:__ Set Intentions and Goals Before you start creating the vision board, take some time to discuss your individual and shared intentions and goals. Write them down and make sure you have a clear comprehension of what you want to manifest in your lives.

Step 4: *Choose Images and Words Start flipping through the magazines and choose images and words that resonate with your intentions and goals. You can cut out pictures of things you want to get, or quotes that inspire you.*

Step 5: *Arrange and Glue*

Arrange the images and words on the poster board or canvas in a way that feels aesthetically pleasing to you. You can create separate sections for individual goals or mix them all together. Once you have arranged everything the way you want it, glue or tape the images and words onto the board.

Step 6: *Display and Visualize Once your vision board is complete, find a prominent place to display it in your home where you can see it every day. Take time to visualize your goals and intentions as you look at the board.*

Step 7: *Review and Update Periodically review your vision board together to see how much progress you have made towards your goals. Celebrate your successes and make updates as needed to reflect any changes in your aspirations or life circumstances.*

Making a vision board can be a fun and engaging activity that allows you to share your dreams and goals with each other. It's also a powerful tool for manifesting your intentions and bringing them to life. Give it a try and see what magic unfolds!

Write Your Sentiments

Chapter 7

Pushing Ahead after Unfaithfulness

Stage 1: Recognize the unfaithfulness

Plunk down with your accomplice and recognize the unfaithfulness

Examine how it has impacted both of you genuinely

Express your sentiments and worries about the fate of the relationship

Stage 2: Assume liability

The accomplice who deceived should assume a sense of ownership with their activities and recognize the hurt they have caused

They should likewise respond to any inquiries their accomplice might have about the disloyalty

The accomplice who was undermined ought to likewise assume a sense of ownership with their own feelings and activities, and work towards pardoning

Stage 3: Lay out limits and assumptions

Talk about what limits and assumptions you each have for the eventual fate of the relationship

Put down clear stopping points to keep any further betrayal from happening

Figure out what moves should be initiated to reconstruct trust and keep up with the relationship

Stage 4: Look for proficient assistance

Think about looking for help from a couples specialist or guide to manage the repercussions of the treachery

A specialist can help you impart really and give devices to modifying trust and mending

Stage 5: Spotlight on revamping trust

Reconstructing trust takes time and exertion from the two accomplices

Make an arrangement for revamping trust and work towards it together

Center around open correspondence, genuineness, and being reliable in your activities

Write Your Thoughts

Reconnecting after Unfaithfulness

Stage 1: Recognize the unfaithfulness and express feelings

Plunk down with your accomplice and recognize the betrayal

Express the way that it has caused you to feel and what feelings you are encountering

Permit your accomplice to do likewise and listen effectively

Stage 2: Assume liability

The accomplice who deceived should get a sense of ownership with their activities and recognize the hurt they have caused

They should likewise respond to any inquiries their accomplice might have about the disloyalty

The accomplice who was undermined ought to likewise get a sense of ownership with their own feelings and activities, and work towards pardoning

Stage 3: Revamp closeness

Reconstructing closeness takes time and exertion from the two accomplices

Begin with little motions, like clasping hands or snuggling, to remake actual closeness

Center around profound closeness by imparting contemplations and sentiments to one another

Stage 4: Practice pardoning

Pardoning is a cycle and takes time

Practice pardoning by recognizing the hurt and agony brought about by the disloyalty, yet in addition by deciding to relinquish pessimistic feelings and hatred

Zero in on pushing ahead and making a positive future together

Stage 5: Lay out new examples and schedules

Make new schedules and examples to build up the trust and association in the relationship

Put away opportunity for date evenings, quality time, and open correspondence

Center around the present and the future, instead of choosing not to move on.

Write Your Thoughts

Revamping Closeness
Worksheet

Recognize the hurt and betrayal: *The two accomplices need to recognize the hurt and agony that the disloyalty caused. This should be possible by having a transparent discussion about how each accomplice feels and what they need from the other to push ahead.*

Make a place of refuge: *The accomplice who duped needs to make a place of refuge for their accomplice to communicate their feelings and concerns. This incorporates showing restraint, listening effectively, and not becoming cautious.*

Be straightforward: *The accomplice who duped should be straightforward and open with their accomplice about their whereabouts, correspondence, and exercises. This can assist with remaking trust over the long haul.*

Put down stopping points: *The two accomplices need to lay out clear limits to keep any further betrayal from happening. This can incorporate things like restricting correspondence with individuals who might represent a gamble to the relationship.*

Revamp closeness: *The two accomplices need to cooperate to remake closeness in the relationship. This can incorporate things like setting aside some margin for date evenings, communicating love, and investigating each other's necessities and wants.*

Write Your Thoughts

Taking care of Oneself

Assume liability: The accomplice who deceived needs to get a sense of ownership with their activities and the aggravation they caused. This incorporates saying 'sorry' genuinely and being willing to offer to set things straight.

Look for guiding: The two accomplices ought to think about looking for directing or treatment to deal with the fallout of unfaithfulness. This can give a place of refuge to communicate feelings, process the experience, and work on reconstructing the relationship.

Center around taking care of oneself: The two accomplices need to focus on taking care of oneself during this time. This can incorporate things like getting sufficient rest, eating great, working out, and rehearsing care or reflection.

Relinquish fault and disdain: The two accomplices need to chip away at relinquishing fault and hatred towards one another. This should be possible by rehearsing pardoning and zeroing in on the future as opposed to choosing not to move on.

Reconnect with leisure activities and interests: The two accomplices ought to find opportunity to reconnect with side interests and interests they appreciate. This can give a feeling of uniqueness and satisfaction beyond the relationship.

Write Your Thoughts

Communication is the Enchanted Thing

This might appear like an easy decision; however, as a platitude by Khalil Gibran goes, "Between what is said and not implied and what is implied and not expressed, the greater part of affection is lost."

You might be thinking about brushing off-base in your relationship under a floor covering to keep up with the deception of a tranquil climate. Yet, the apparent issue will become more excellent. Gulping your tongue won't make the aggravation disappear, and neither one of the wills become suddenly angry or retribution. However much it feels like you are returning injuries from a long time ago and remembering your aggravation, sound correspondence is the primary movement on the most proficient method to fabricate trust in connections. Make time to do the accompanying correspondence exercises. Ensure that your partner doesn't hinder you while you talk;

• Tell your partner how you feel about the circumstances that caused you to lose trust in them.

• Make sense of why these ways of behaving have harmed you. (Let it all out, regardless of how immaterial you might be convinced to think what is happening that harms you is. Enlightening your partner can open the entryways of acknowledgment and assist you with pinpointing when these ways of behaving started to hurt you and in what capacity.)

• Express how you want your partner to make you trust them once more. (Be it giving you space, being more present, not scrutinizing your world and causing you to feel tiny, or being more grounded close to home and monetary help.)

After this, give them the floor to talk.

Focus on their non-verbal communication and words. Does your partner appear to be repentant? Do they feel ownership of the hurt they have caused you? Do they appear to be prepared to take the necessary steps to revamp trust?

Support Consistent Correspondence

Another significant hint while investing the effort into exercises to reconstruct trust in a relationship is to recollect that you can't tackle all your trust issues in a day.

Approach it slowly and carefully, trying to give yourself breaks when you feel yourself blowing up or contrite.

As you uncover the hurt, you or your partner might need to stay away from any further correspondence, yet this will cause more damage than great. In the event that you are off base, taking off might make things somewhat worse. Keep in mind both parties deserve equal credit here. Correspondence, as recently examined, is an or more. However, in instances of unfaithfulness, it is best not to delve into subtleties, particularly without the presence and guidance of an authorized specialist. A specialist can give an unbiased examination with respect to whether you both are correct or wrong.

Despite the fact that your partner might need to know each and every detail and strain you to spill the complexities of your disloyalty, doing so will be counterproductive and give no solace to your partner. It will just make it harder to relinquish now that they can picture the occasion. Also, while attempting to make sense of it, you might wind up saying something embarrassing and offering something that will make your partner discharge up. There could be no other result. For this reason, seeing a specialist and having them intervene in your meetings will assist with the justification behind your unfaithfulness, in addition, assist you with conveying your considerations to your partner in a better and more open manner. This carries us to the following point.

Pardoning Will Liberate You

You might be searching for trust-building worksheets for couples. However, I'll stop you there to remind you what is beating the rundown of exercises to modify trust in a relationship: pardoning. At the point when a partner undermines you or when you start to feel like the individual they were, the point at which you created your relationship is, as now, not the individual they are present, you might begin to fault yourself.

If you are off base and can't excuse yourself for what you did, this fault can prompt anguish, uneasiness, dietary problems, and culpability disorder.

To come above water, you must excuse yourself and pardon your partner. Follow these tips;

• Recall that you do it for your advantage when you excuse yourself and your partner. Pardoning breaks you liberated from the shackles of the past.

• Pardoning allows your partner to right their wrongs and gain from their mix-ups.

Chapter 8

30+ Tips and Tricks for Recovering affair In a Relationship

Fortunately even after an overwhelming double-crossing like cheating, trust can be rebuilt.5 Not just that, selling out is in many cases the impetus for restoring a relationship that was in some hot water well before the disloyalty happened. Recuperating is an excursion, yet when two individuals are profoundly dedicated to grasping, offering to set things right, and committing once again, sorcery can occur.

The following are twenty methods for reconstructing trust in a relationship:

Commit a Responsibility

The two partners need to commit 100 percent to accomplishing the work engaged with mending after a double-crossing. It is a drawn out venture, contingent upon the sort of selling out, yet feeling the relationship merits battling for is the responsibility the two partners need to make.

The two Partners Assume Liability

Responsibility from the traitor implies demonstrating to your partner that you are genuinely grieved and ready to chip away at procuring back trust, regardless of the stuff. Responsibility from the double-crossed includes undivided attention to the deceiver along with investigating any of their own ways of behaving that might have added to trouble in the relationship before the betrayal.5

Refine Your Correspondence Style

Asking your partner unassuming inquiries is an incredible method for expanding profound closeness and revamp trust. It cultivates personal exchange since these inquiries can't be responded to with a straightforward "Yes" or "No." How you decide to convey complaints matters. Figuring out how to self-relieve can permit both the speaker and the audience to endure the pressure to handle the selling out.

Acknowledge Fix Endeavors

Remaking trust generally boils down to concluding whether you need vengeance or a relationship. Worldwide marriage specialists expresses that after an earnest conciliatory sentiment is given, when deceived partners don't acknowledge fix endeavors, there is an expanded gamble of divorce.

Put down a Point in time to Discuss the Selling out

It's vital to set a day to day time (15-20 minutes) to discuss the disloyalty; any other way, it could be a day in and day out conversation. This permits each partner to get ready for a useful conversation along with oversee any feelings that might emerge out of the blue. Assess progress week after week to know when to diminish the recurrence of the gatherings.

Set Time for a Non-Debatable Week by week Marriage Meeting

A week by week marriage meeting is an extraordinary custom to fortify a partnership. This is a devoted chance frankly and convey about central questions in the relationship. Great subjects to examine incorporate appreciation, things that did/turned out poorly throughout the span of the week (in a non-basic and non-guarded way), tasks, funds, outside responsibilities, date evenings, and so forth.

Reclassify New Marriage Rules

Having purposeful standards can assist the sold out partner with feeling a feeling of control while reconstructing trust. Self inflicted rules are liberating since they are non-debatable and grown together. These can include defining sound relationship limits and everyday registrations to restrict issues from heightening.

Make a Culture of Appreciation

Couples who track down ways of communicating appreciation for one another frequently have a more noteworthy opportunity to fix broken trust. This is tied in with sharing a "we-ness" or harmony versus a separateness. Praising the battle implies communicating pride that you've endure significant difficulties in your relationship. Effectively discussing your obligation to each other as opposed to addressing whether you pursued the best decision is instrumental in remaking trust.

Shut down All Contact with the Undertaking Partner

Assuming there is still contact with the undertaking partner, recuperation will be significantly postponed. This implies finishing all physical, close to home, and verbal closeness. On the off chance that the undertaking partner is a collaborator, the contact should be rigorously business.

Share Any Important or Spontaneous Experiences with the Undertaking Partner

This implies there is a climate of full straightforwardness assuming that undeniable contact with the undertaking partner must be made. This shows up with a readiness to transparently respond to any inquiries your partner might have.

Try not to Chatter About or Junk Talk Your Partner to Other people

Meddling and waste talking make an additional layer of pressure, particularly when the objective is to chip away at your relationship. It very well may be enticing to vent or need to vent, yet it comes down to realizing that what you center around grows, so pick who you converse with and how you discuss your partner astutely.

Recount the Genuine Story of the Treachery

Recounting the account of the issue is difficult for one or the other partner, yet it will offer you and your partner a chance to comprehend what occurred and why. The harmed partner genuinely must doesn't participate in a damaging course of cross examination and preventiveness, which never advances recuperating, regardless of whether the responses are honest. All things considered, start with tending to the straightforward facts.

Establish Climate of Proactive Straight forwardness

Our feelings can hinder coming clean and hearing reality. Straightforwardness keeps everything out in the open to work with trust and quit overthinking in the relationship. Proactive straightforwardness includes putting forth the extra attempt to feature significant things about the double-crossing without ready to be tested or inquired. This forms trust and shows a preparation to be held accountable.8

Figure out the Force of Weakness

In being defenseless, you can make a degree of profound security with your partner. It's the essential method for reinforcing a conjugal bond and keep love alive. It's the way you'll have the option to restore a safe profound connection and protect closeness in your marriage. This remains forever inseparable with proactive straightforwardness.

Assess Your Inquiries

To pose helpful inquiries, the deceived partner necessities to stop and consider. Great inquiries include thinking about how your inquiry will assist with understanding what occurred and why it worked out. The objective is to pose smart inquiries that brief productive responses.9

Likely inquiries to pose to yourself prior to asking your partner:

Is the response something I truly need to be aware?

Is the response something that will help in my recuperation?

Is this question something that will not be useful?

Will it fuel meddling contemplations and triggers?

Assess Your Responses

The traitor needs to respond to any inquiries honestly, yet in addition with the most minimal degree of detail conceivable. The objective is to try not to any upset pictures the deceived may need to manage later on. Swindling has been related with side effects like post-horrendous pressure problem (PTSD) and double-crossing injury, so such a large number of realistic subtleties might put a weight on the recuperating system.

Carve out opportunity to Pardon

It requires investment to really comprehend the reason why a disloyalty occurred, so stopping the recuperating system won't consider viable recuperation to happen. At the end of the day, evasion is never a technique for mending, nor is excusing too early. Building a safe attachment to your partner implies taking however much time as could be expected to completely process and work on better survival methods to reconstruct the relationship.

Allow Persistence to prepare

Assuming you are off base, you can't get disappointed with your partner when they appear to be angry with you. You want to comprehend that your partner is harmed and they need consolation from you.

Your partner must be aware, with no proportion of sensible uncertainty, that you won't break their trust again. This moment isn't the opportunity to toss it right in front of them that you are attempting to make things work or fire up at their reluctance to show you the affection you underestimated.

It is not necessarily the case that they ought to rebuff you or cause you to languish over years to come. Be that as it may, try to show the three p's;

• Tolerance

• Steadiness

• Presence

Be Ready For A Swing Of Feelings

As you work on the most proficient method to remake trust after cheating, you should prepare yourself for many feelings. Similarly, as how swings go this way and at different rates, you might see a similar about how you feel.

Every so often, you might feel like you are fine; you recall the double-crossing on different days. Occasionally you might think you have excused your partner or yourself; other days, you put yourself down. Recollect that time, recuperates all injuries, and never shut your partner out. Continuously let them in on your feelings, and never avoid looking for proficient help.

Agree with Admittance to Your Partner's phone

Allowing your partner to go through your telephone is only sometimes bright. Having a good sense of security is significant for building a profound association and, afterward, trust.

In any case, there are discussions between companions that might be so touchy they feel awkward enough telling your partner about them. So to glance through your telephone is intensely attacking someone else's security. You are likewise qualified for your pride and space, personally.

To construct trust again with somebody who undermined you, continually expecting to see their telephones won't assist with your tension or trust-working by any means. Here are a few guidelines regarding calls and web-based entertainment that can cause your partner to feel great;

• Assuming your partner who you undermined needs you to stay away from the individual you cheated with or somebody they are not happy with, you would have to stick to that.

This shows that you are tuning in and prepared to encourage your partner around you again.

• Try not to like pictures of individuals that cause your partner to feel shaky. On the off chance that your partner has a few substantial uncertainties about their body, enjoying views of two-piece models or, on account of a man, solid male competitors can cause the three d's that should be kept away from while attempting to fabricate a place of refuge: dysmorphia, gloom, and distrust.

• Set your particular standards and guidelines regarding wireless use, for example, when the telephones ought to be placed away for one-on-time.

• Never go behind your partner by defying these telephone guidelines. Sneaking around shows you are untrustworthy and have no faith in your partner. Sneaking around will make a poisonous cycle, and that feeling of safety that relies vigorously upon telephone access will sink your relationship.

Send Your Partner on Little Tasks

While your partner is out or taken off, advise them to assist you with getting something quite specific — maybe a brand of body item or a food thing you want. Doing so allows your partner to show you that you can trust them to show up for you in every one of the little ways that matter. Advise your partner to get your number one brand of frozen yogurt on their way from work or the exercise center and to call or message you if the thing isn't accessible. This is in no way trying to control your partner or test them. However, it is a way for them to procure your trust with extra care.

Share Your Weaknesses and Fears

At the point when your walls or your partner's walls are up, closeness can not flourish. Conversing with your partner about your uncertainties and fears won't just permit your partner to comfort you and feel nearer to you, yet it will help you to feel more secure with one another.

Be Your Partner's Guardian

Following your and your partner's discussions about your apprehensions and uncertainties, you both should comprehend that this data is classified. This data should never become visible without your partner's consent, particularly as a joke. This classifies as a break of your trust and can fix some of the work you both have done to make your relationship sail without a hitch. While investigating how to fabricate trust in a relationship once more, you should recollect these tips. Huge news and other significant data your partner imparts to you, for example, pregnancy or advancement, ought to be left well enough alone until they are prepared to share it, notwithstanding your perspectives. If you feel like you can't hold it in any longer, trust these feelings in your partner or a diary, as opposed to another relative or companion.

Have Your Partner's Back When Others Are Available

Work on having your partner's back when you are out of the house or when visitors are finished. Save conflicts till you are in private; then, you can freshen up your sentiments with them. It will appear to be agreeing with another person's position when there is a conflict or somebody is, by all accounts putting your partner down, professing to be kidding. Rather than supporting your partner, you participate or stay silent. It isn't being phony since going to bat for your partner will cause them to have a solid sense of security and cherish. These feelings will go far towards reconstructing trust in a relationship and, as an additional motivation, will likewise make your partner more open to your bone of dispute.

Redo A Language

When you start to discuss steadily with your partner, you both will comprehend that there are a few words you and your partner utter or ways of behaving you and the partner show that might set off both of you. Concurring upon an expression or a signal that will tell your partner when you are severely or feeling outraged will go miles towards remaking trust in a relationship.

Make New Firsts

Another of the exercises to modify trust in a relationship is to make new and better recollections with your partner by attempting new things interestingly. The key is to keep a receptive outlook; Is there something you or your partner have at any point needed to attempt? Like going to a chocolate production class, a music show, a play, or in any event, going bungee hopping? Try not to thump down your partner's thoughts; however, allow the floor to be open for feelings, and you very well could track down another holding movement.

In conclusion, recollect that you don't need to be the triumphant couple or the most assembled; the objective is to have loads of tomfoolery and construct closeness and trust.

Be a Shoulder to Rest On

When your partner goes through a difficult stretch, you might think the arrangement is directly before their face. In any case, what you see as straightforward is much more troublesome from their perspective.

Instead of attempting to be an educator or a parent who pushes them towards change, realize that it is a cycle that takes time.

Be Their Umbrella

When the downpour comes pouring down, umbrellas resemble a familiar object, making the problematic stretches less overwhelming. Be an emotionally supportive network that reminds your partner they are in good company. Couples' or one-on-one treatment is likewise an incredible put to carry on the mending system.

Never Acknowledge Misuse

However much you might need to show up for going through extreme individual times, you should define the boundary regarding forfeiting your joy. Close to home and actual maltreatment ought never to be endured.

Suppose your partner is continually checking or tapping your telephone, criticizing you, blaming you for cheating, and keeping you from having any companions of the other gender. In that case, this is a poisonous way of behaving. Assuming your partner keeps you from heading outside, will not accommodate you monetarily, or, more terribly, lays their hands on you, you want to get away from that relationship. Never be so centered around what someone else is going through that you imperil or forfeit your genuine serenity, bliss, and security. You are not their close-to-home punching pack or mat; however, you are an individual they should regard and see as their equivalent.

Be a Portrayal of the Trust You Look for

You can't search for trust in that frame of mind while they don't have a good sense of security with or around you. Similarly, as regard is equal, faith is as well.

At the point when you say you will follow through with something, keep to your promise. Neglecting to get them something you vowed to or to call at a settled time may appear tiny to you; however, it is an immense arrangement. Counting persistence, trustworthiness, and unwavering quality towards your partner usually pushes them towards trusting you and responding to your feelings.

Never Let Sentiment Wilt

Essential signals like getting blossoms and chocolates, another tie for your partner, or something they referenced in passing will go far toward causing them to feel loved.

Look for Proficient Assistance

Frequently, a couple is overpowered to the point that they don't have the foggiest idea where to start. This is where a couple's instructor can be instrumental. They can direct both the sold out and the deceiver to ask and respond to inquiries in a manner that works with recuperation. They can direct couples with structure and a game plan to dial back the most common way of mending to a valuable speed.

Plan, Plan, Plan

Cooperate to foster an arrangement to forestall further breaks of trust. Be available to recognizing regions that might have made mistrust (keeping monetary data, not sharing data in your day to day living, investing a lot of energy beyond the relationship, and so on). Plan to increment fellowship, make ceremonies of association, and fabricate another relationship together.

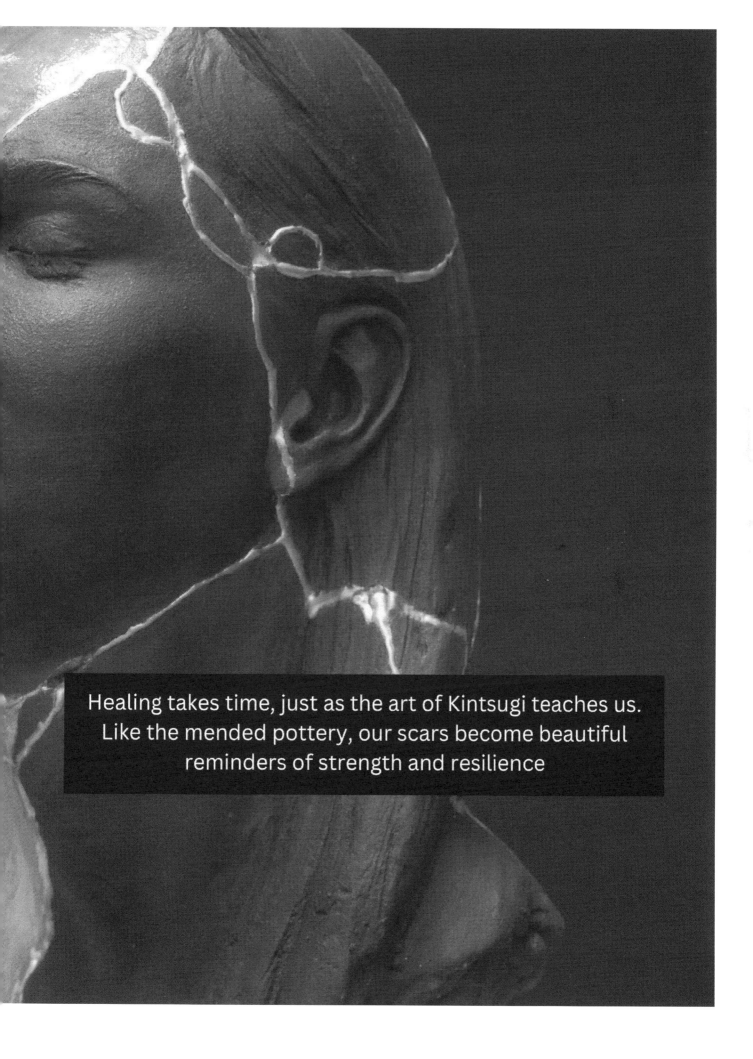

Healing takes time, just as the art of Kintsugi teaches us. Like the mended pottery, our scars become beautiful reminders of strength and resilience

Final Thought

The journey to recover after affair can be a difficult and emotional one, but with the right mindset and guidance, couples can overcome obstacles and come out stronger on the other side. By implementing the tips and techniques outlined in this book, couples can work towards restoring trust and rebuilding their relationship. We hope that this book has been a valuable resource for those looking to rebuild trust in their relationship. It's never too late to start working towards a healthier, more fulfilling partnership, and we believe that this book can provide the guidance and support needed to get there. We encourage our readers to continue learning and growing in their relationships, and we look forward to providing more resources and support in the future.

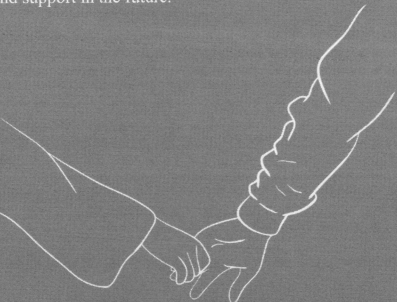

Thank You for reading this Book!

I hope you enjoyed reading my book!

Made in United States
Troutdale, OR
11/21/2023